Private Worship

THE KEY TO JOY

NANCY
MISSLER

KHW

Private Worship: The Key to Joy

Copyright 2002 by Nancy Missler

Published by *The King's High Way* Ministries
P.O. Box 3111
Coeur d'Alene, ID 83816
http: www.kingshighway.org

Second Printing, October 2003

ISBN: 0-9745177-1-2

All Scripture quotations are from the King James Version
of the Holy Bible.

Cover design by David Clemens, Coeur d'Alene, ID
Inside illustrations by Lynae Minnich, Newport, WA.

PRINTED IN THE UNITED STATES OF AMERICA

Table of Contents

"Thou hast made known to me the ways of life; Thou shalt make me full of joy with Thy countenance."

Acts 2:28

Foreword

Sooner or later, all journeys must end. And it's only right in the grand experiment of life that this be so. After all, only the fool travels merely for the sake of traveling. The warm home, late night talks with old and valued friends, the restful bed in familiar surroundings, relaxation in that certain place that seems to have been made just for us—these are the rightful rewards for enduring the dangers of the journey.

And the journey of life **must** lead us Home to that certain place that really has been tailor made just for us, if I read Christ's words in John 14:2 aright. God's "house of many mansions"—to use that old King James term—is ringed with many townhouses, each of them lovingly crafted from before the foundation of the world by a wise and omnipotent Architect.

These rooms have been custom-designed to house the souls of each one of God's Elect. And our hearts are restless, Christian believers of long ago have reminded us, until they find their rest in Him.

Now I think the real challenge we Christians face all too often is how to find our way home in this life.

Frankly, it's just not possible unless you understand how to find joy on the journey. And that's where Nancy Missler's edifying book **Private Worship: The Key to Joy** finds its rightful place in the Christian's library. By reading this book, I am reminded—I always knew it to be true, I just tend to forget it too easily—that the place of worship is the place of rest on that symbolic journey called the Christian life.

Nancy Missler's insightful volume is the culmination of her insightful trilogy that began with **The Way of Agape**, continued on with **Be Ye Transformed**, and then concluded with the problem of how to have **Faith in the Night Seasons** of life. Or at least I thought the trilogy concluded with **Faith in the Night Seasons**. As it turns out, **Private Worship: The Key to Joy** is where the journey of **Faith in the Night Seasons** will rightfully end.

Several principles keep coming to mind as I read **Private Worship: The Key to Joy**. Here are four of them:

1. The first requirement for being effective in your Christian life is to remember that only those who love God will serve him with joy.
2. But only those who know how to worship Him can successfully contain that joy.
3. Jesus Himself warned five of the seven pastors to the

churches of Revelation 2-3 that various sins of omission or commission can lead to a flaccid spirituality. But all of these sins can result in a quiet refusal to worship Him. And that leads to ***uselessness***.

4. If heaven is our destined home, worship is our destined pastime. As a result, now is the season of time in which we must learn how to do it effectively.

Private Worship: The Key to Joy is one of the finest resources I've read to date that can serve as a practical guide on helping all of us learn how to return to the love we had at the first. So come back home by reading Nancy Missler's ***Private Worship: The Key to Joy***. Come home to worship. It's the place where you belong. You always have belonged there. And deep inside your heart you know that's true. You belong there. Forever. It's the place of Joy. You were made for it.

If you've lost your way for a season, maybe because your faith has been tested in the darkness of night, Nancy's ***Private Worship: The Key to Joy*** may be just the thing to set you back on the straight and narrow. For worship of our great God truly is the key to joy.

William Welty

William P. Welty, M.Div.
Executive Director of The ISV Foundation
Translators of the Holy Bible: International Standard Version®

Introduction

Worship is the single most important thing a Christian can learn to do.

A.W. Tozer once wrote, "Why did Christ come? Why was He conceived? Why was He born? Why was He crucified? Why did He rise again? Why is He now at the right hand of the Father?" The answer to all of these questions, Tozer says, is: *"...in order that He might make worshipers out of rebels."*[1]

Worship is what distinguishes the Church from the world. When we worship, God's presence ceases to be something we only talk about and, instead, becomes a personal experience out of which we build an intimate relationship. In other words, worship is an experience by which we touch the unseen. It's a divine encounter that not only brings Him glory, but also unveils His Word a little more clearly to us. Worship not only opens the doorway to God's Love, but also to His revelation and joy.

When do we Worship? *How* do we Worship?

When God put it on my heart to write a book about worship, I questioned my friends, my family and others

---

[1] *Experiencing God in Worship,* page 155.

how and when they worshiped. "Do you worship the Lord on a daily basis, or just on Sundays?" The answers I received were surprising: One friend said, "Oh, I worship the Lord all the time!" Another commented, "I worship when I'm cleaning the house." Another actually replied, "I worship the Lord when I'm with the children." A gentleman responded, "I worship the Lord when I'm driving in the car." Another commented, "I worship Him when I'm at the office"; etc. In other words, the general response I received was *"I worship the Lord all day long, no matter what I'm doing."*

Now, I understand what these believers are saying—they have an *attitude* of worshiping the Lord all day long. And that's fine and that's good, but is that really what God means when He says in John 4:23-24, "The hour cometh, and now is, when the *true worshipers shall worship the Father in spirit and in truth: for the Father seeketh such to worship Him. God is a Spirit: and they that worship Him must worship Him in spirit and in truth."*

In other words, can we really "worship the Lord" while cleaning the house, while being with the children, while driving our cars or being at the office? Is this really what God desires? This is what we want to explore in this little book.

What is worship? How important is it? Do we worship the Lord *only* on Sundays in church or are we to worship Him privately at home every day? If the latter, how do we do it? And, most importantly, how does *God* want us to worship Him?

My Story

Let me start at the beginning:

A few months ago, I was experiencing so many disappointments in my life (those "little foxes" that Song of Songs 2:15 talks about) that I just shut down emotionally. I simply disengaged. It was as if the life in me just drained out. I think our physical body instinctively knows how to defend itself from more emotional attacks, and it does so by simply shutting down and closing off. And that's exactly what happened to me.

Maybe some of you can relate.

The problem is that when we shut down like this, we also quench God's Life (in our hearts) as well. I felt as if His Life in me wasn't just quenched or blocked, it was gone completely. The joy of my salvation had completely evaporated. I continued going about my daily business— Bible studies, prayer, fellowship—but it was almost by rote, mechanical at best.

The scary part to me was that I was daily making all the right "faith" choices: I was confessing my sin and self, repenting of those things, giving myself totally over to the Lord and choosing to walk by faith. (I've been teaching these principles and doing them personally for over twenty years.) But this time, something was really very wrong because my feelings were not aligning with my faith choices (as they always have in the past), and the really frightening part was that the joy of my salvation wasn't returning!

No matter how much I prayed, confessed, repented and gave things to God, I remained shut down, with absolutely *no joy*. I so identified with Proverbs 17:22 which says, "...a broken spirit drieth the bones." In the Living Translation the words are, *a crushed spirit saps our strength*. It's so true: when we are really spiritually depressed, *everything* in our life is affected. It's almost as if our blood supply is dried up. It frightened me because: how can I teach these cleansing and renewing principles to others if they're not working in my own life?

Those who know me well saw right through my forced outward smile and were very concerned. Others saw my grin and were oblivious to my hidden struggle.

But *I* knew something was terribly wrong. Either God wasn't who He said He was, and walking by faith doesn't really work (which I knew in my heart wasn't true), <u>or</u>, He was again "cornering me" to teach me something new. (All of my previous books have come about through personal experiences that the Lord has allowed in my life to teach me His ways. My books are simply a chronology of my walk with Him over the last 25 years.) So I began praying that this might be the case here also.

It was interesting because the very week that all of this was going on, two different people—unexpectedly and out of the blue—prayed that God would give me "new revelation" for the next book that God would call me to write. That became my prayer also.

There's that Word, "Worship"

During the second week that I was in this horrible state of mind, I picked up an article that actually was intended for Chuck but had mistakenly come across my desk. I casually began reading it over when one word in the first paragraph absolutely leaped out at me: *worship*!

The article, entitled *Tired of a Tired Pastor,* by Francis Frangipane. This is what I read:

"In the early 1970s, during the beginning of my ministry, the Lord called me to consecrate to Him the time from dawn until noon. I spent these hours in prayer, *worship* and the study of His Word. I would often worship God for hours, writing songs of Him that came from this wonderful sanctuary of love. The presence of the Lord was my delight, and I know my time with Him was not only well-spent, but well-pleasing to us both.

"However, as my life began to bear the fruit of Christ's influence, the Holy Spirit would bring people to me for ministry. In time, as more people would come, I found myself cutting off forty-five minutes from the end of my devotional time. On occasion, ministry to people would extend into the night, and I stopped rising as early as I had.

"Church growth problems began to eat at the quality of my remaining time; ministerial expansion, training younger ministries and more counseling crowded the already limited time I had left. Of course, these changes did not happen overnight, but the months and years of increasing success were steadily eroding my devotional life. In time I found myself in a growing ministry but with a shrinking anointing to sustain it.

"One day an intercessor called who prayed regularly for me. He told me that during the night the Lord had spoken to him in a dream concerning me. I was eager to hear what the Lord had revealed to my friend, thinking perhaps He was going to increase our outreach or maybe supply some needed finances. I asked him to tell me the dream.

"What the Lord said had nothing directly to do with the projects and the priorities that were consuming my time. He simply said, 'Tell Francis I miss him.'"

The author went on to say that he had become so tired and so dry from doing the Lord's work that he needed to get back to reading the Word more, praying more and *worshiping the Lord more.*

"Worshiping the Lord more"? I thought for a moment. Do I really worship the Lord? I know I pray, I know I praise and I know I read the Word, but do I really worship Him? My mind continued to race, "How is worshiping God any different from praising Him or from blessing Him? In fact, what does it really mean to worship?

The rest of the evening, I continued this line of personal questioning: Is worship something we do just in church on Sundays, something we do all day long (at the office, in the car, etc.), or are we to personally worship the Lord in some special way *daily* at home? And, if that's the case, how exactly do we do that? These questions plagued my mind all night long. How would *you* answer these questions?

No Joy

The next day, I was in the office with the head of our prayer ministry and, unexpectedly, she showed me a letter from a woman who was concerned about her daughter losing "the joy of her salvation." As I read the letter, the Lord totally convicted me, because that letter perfectly described my life *at that moment*!

Many things had happened in this young woman's life (just as they had in mine) that had left her almost "shell-shocked." The mother wrote that her daughter "is there in body only, but with absolutely no emotions and no joy." And, of course, that was exactly how I felt! She said it was tearing her family up because none of them was able to minister to her. Then she closed her letter by saying, "Please, can you help us..."

I left the prayer office in total shock, because I knew exactly what that young woman was experiencing. How, Lord, I thought, does one restore his joy? (No matter how hard we try, I know it's impossible to change our own feelings. There's no way we can manufacture them, hype them up or counterfeit them.) So, what is the answer, Lord? I walked away from my friend's office feeling totally helpless and even more confused than ever, with all these unanswered questions racing in my mind.

That afternoon in my daily reading of the Word, I came to Psalm 65:4, "What joy awaits us inside Your Holy Temple." (New Living Translation) The word *joy* caught my attention and I found it fascinating that it was somehow connected to God's Holy Temple. Lord, I cried, what are You trying to show me through all of this?

God's Voice

The event that finally put everything into perspective, and sparked a whole new level in my spiritual walk, happened later that night. After dinner, I sat down to finish my Bible reading and I happened to be in Luke 4, which talks about the three temptations of Christ. As you may recall, Christ's rebuttal to Satan in the third temptation is that we should *worship* and serve the Lord only: "Thou shalt *worship* the Lord thy God, and Him only shalt thou serve." Wow! There's that word *worship* again, I thought, which automatically propelled the same line of questioning:

Lord, do I worship You? I know I praise You; I know I pray to You; and, I know I read Your Word; but do I really worship You?

God's answer to me was almost audible, *"You don't even know what worship means, and that's why you have no joy!"*

My mind raced: What are You saying, Lord? Worship and joy are linked? How?

God began to lovingly unfold His wisdom to me. He first showed me that, *yes*, I had been praising Him;

and, *yes*, I had been confessing and repenting my sins; and, *yes*, I had been reading His Word. But, after I did these things I would get up and go about my business, without so much as a thought about *worshiping Him*. Oh yes, every once in a while, I would raise my hands in church or fall on my face to pray for something specific or cry if I heard a moving tape, but He showed me that I had never really entered into worshiping Him and adoring Him on a daily or personal basis. The truth was I didn't really know how!

As a result of all of this, I had lost the joy of my salvation and my spiritual strength had evaporated.

Only "in Thy presence, is fulness of joy...", Psalm 16:11 tells us.

Course of Action

God has called me to be a teacher and I absolutely love the "treasure hunts" that He puts me on. After the above encounter with Him, I got out every book, every commentary, every Bible translation, every Bible dictionary and every concordance that I could find about *worship* and about *joy*. The first night, I literally stayed up all night, lost in my quest for understanding. I was determined to find out what He meant when He says, "Worship Me." *How* are we supposed to worship Him? And finally, how is joy tied to worship?

I was aware of the above Psalm 16:11, but I never realized that worship is really the only "key" that opens the door to His presence. In other words, being before Him in *worship* leads to His presence and thus, to fulness of joy. I never put these together. This realization also brings Nehemiah 8:10 into better perspective: "...the joy of the Lord is our strength." What this means is: *without worship (without being in His presence), we will have no joy; and without joy, we will have no strength.* Our life's blood will dry up, and we'll wither and die spiritually.

This is so true. Look at the body of believers today. As a whole, we are joyless, powerless and loveless. Why? Because we are not worshipers! We don't worship the Father *in spirit and in truth.* In reality, most of us worship other things (other people, careers, sports, fame, wealth, etc.). We put these things first in our lives, not the Lord. This is why Tozer, in the quote on the first page, intimated that *learning to worship the Lord is the most important thing a Christian can do. It's the key to His presence and thus, to our happiness.*

After my encounter with the Lord, I was hooked. I was determined, at all costs, to find out *what* authentic worship really is; *how* we are supposed to worship; and *when* are we supposed to worship.

This little book will attempt to explore some of the incredible things that the Lord is showing me and how they are changing my life...

What is Worship -
Why is it so Important?

Definition of Worship

Worship simply means *a divine encounter with God.*

Worship comes from love. Where love is deep, worship will overflow. In other words, we really can't worship the Lord, unless we love Him. This is why worship is often called "the language of love." It's the means by which love flows from a believer back to the Lord. It's bringing the *Agape* Love that Christ originally put in our hearts when we were first born again, full circle back to Him in adoration and exaltation.

The Greek word for worship is *proskuneo,* which means to bow down, stoop down, fall down, adore, show absolute reverence, homage or submission. It means to *kiss, to prostrate oneself* or touch one's nose to the ground. Throughout Scripture you will see how the saints always "fell on their faces," bowed down or prostrated themselves before the Lord when they worshiped.

In the Old Testament, 2 Chronicles 7:3 tells us "...when all the children of Israel saw how the fire came down, and the glory of the LORD upon the house, they bowed themselves with their faces to the ground upon the pavement, and worshiped, and praised the LORD..." In the New Testament, Revelation 4:10 exclaims, "The four and twenty elders fall down before Him that sat on the throne, and worship Him that liveth for ever and ever, and cast their crowns before the throne." (See also Revelation 5:8, 14; 19:10; 1 Corinthians 14:25.)

Worshiping means extolling, magnifying, glorifying, exalting, honoring and celebrating the Lord. *Proskuneo* is something that is done on the "inside"—in our spirit—defined by Jesus in John 4:23-24: "...the true worshipers shall worship the Father in spirit and in truth." Worshiping in the spirit is prostrating and bowing down our inner man before the Lord. It's asking nothing of Him, but losing ourselves in adoration, reverence and homage.

The definition of worship that I really like is that worship means *to catch fire*. I can almost visualize catching fire with the Love of God! When something catches on fire, it is literally *consumed by it*. This is exactly what happens in worship. We become consumed in our love for the Lord and *one* in spirit with Him. It's a uniting or a becoming one of two separate spirits. It's a binding of ourselves or a joining of ourselves to the object of our love. God is a Spirit and only that which is spirit can abide in His presence. Thus, worshiping the Lord "in the spirit" means adoring, praising and loving Him *in the same nature as He is*—in the Spirit.

This kind of worship can happen even in our darkest hour. It can happen even when life seems hopeless, even when all we can do is affirm our love and His Lordship.

Worship, then, is simply an act of our heart—it's being so overwhelmed by the revelation of God's Love, that we respond in unabashed loving gratitude. Our external act of prostration simply denotes our "inward" spiritual attitude of love, meekness and reverence.

King David is a perfect example of one who truly worshiped the Lord. Listen to Psalm 63:1-4 as an expression of His love: "O God, thou art my God; early will I seek Thee: my soul thirsteth for Thee, my flesh longeth for Thee in a dry and thirsty land, where no water is; To see Thy power and Thy *glory*, so as I have seen Thee in the sanctuary. Because *Thy lovingkindness is better than life*, my lips shall praise Thee. Thus will I bless Thee while I live: I will lift up my hands in Thy name."

David had a passionate love for God and desired, more than anything else, to know His presence in His life. Because David was so confident that God loved him, he was able to continually surrender and yield his own life.

Do we worship the Lord like this? Do we daily, like David, surrender our lives and prostrate ourselves before Him?

George Barna, the famous author and statistician says, "Virtually every church in the nation provides opportunities for worship, yet, *we rarely really worship God. Most Christians admit they seldom feel like they have connected with Him.*"

Most believers know that they have a responsibility to worship, but when asked to define what true worship means or how to do it, they are unable to offer any answers.

What Makes Worship So Important?

Man has an inbuilt need to express His love and gratitude to some deity and that "someone" determines his worship.

Believers can worship and love the Lord with all their heart and soul because they have already invited Him into their lives. Thus, their spirits have already been made alive and already quickened by His Spirit. John 6:63 validates this: "It is the spirit that quickeneth; the flesh profiteth nothing: the words that I speak unto you, *they* are spirit, and *they* are life."

Non-believers, on the other hand, cannot really worship the Lord this way. They can have a external form of worship, but because their spirits are not united with or quickened by God's Spirit internally, they really cannot communicate or fellowship with the Father. Therefore, they cannot personally or intimately know Him. Listen to John 3:5-6: "Jesus answered, Verily, verily, I say unto thee, Except a man be born of water *and of the spirit*, he cannot enter into the kingdom of God. That which is born of the flesh is flesh; and that which is born of the Spirit is spirit." We often read about a "God-shaped hole" in our hearts. And, it's so true: without an intimate relationship with Christ, nothing on earth will ever fill us.

Though God doesn't need our worship, He *is* seeking those who are worshipers. Thus, one of the reasons we worship is to minister to and bless Him. Worship is the time we concentrate on Christ, not ourselves. It's the time we forget about ourselves and realize and experience *His* presence.

Worship is important because, as Tozer said, "...it's the reason Christ came, the reason He was crucified and the reason He rose again." Furthermore, the entire book of Revelation concerns the importance of worship and what God thinks of worship.   Again, Revelation 4:8-11 is an example: "The four and twenty elders fall down before Him that sat on the throne, and worship Him that liveth for ever and ever, and cast their crowns before the throne, saying, Thou art worthy, O Lord, to receive glory and honour and power: for Thou hast created all things and for Thy pleasure they are and were created."   Other pertinent Revelation Scriptures are Revelation 11:16 and 19:4.

There are also many other Scriptures in the Word that tell us God is seeking true worshipers. Scriptures like Psalm 95:6-7: "Oh, come, let us worship and bow down; let us kneel before the Lord our maker. For He is our God, and we are the people of His pasture, and the sheep of His hand..." And Psalm 99:5, "Exalt ye the LORD our God, and worship at His footstool; for He *is* holy."

Worship is critical because it's what brings us intimacy with the Father. In other words, worship is a two-way communication. We come into His presence by loving, adoring and exalting Him. He then makes Himself known by communicating His Love back to us. This, of course, results in inexpressible joy for us.

This daily communion is what allows us to endure difficult circumstances. If we are hearing from the Lord, we can withstand anything. Thus, worship is the *key* to intimacy, to withstanding trials and problems and to restoring the joy of our salvation.

Our ability to worship is developed through application. In other words, *we learn to worship by worshiping.* The problem is, most of us have not been taught to worship. Sadly, the motivation for most Christians to worship is so that we might have "an enjoyable time"–not solely to honor and please God. Our cultural context has defined our worship services. They are simply an hour where we study the Bible and sharpen our discipleship rather than bringing us face to face with God. In other words, worship has become "horizontal" rather than "vertical," and thus is often made up of ritual without reality, form without power.

Unfortunately, the music in many of our church services is what determines how effective the worship is. This, however, is not what the Word of God says. The Bible tells us that worship is not just to engage the audience, but to *have them change as a result of it.* Consequently, worship that is directed toward entertaining the congregation is not Scriptural worship but simply a form of pleasure and gratification.

The real problem is that many of us don't really have a heart thirsty for more of God, nor do we know how to express our love to Him. We talk about worshiping God, we exhort others to do it and we sing worship songs, but how many of us really, personally worship Him? Most of us don't have the faintest idea of *how* to worship, let alone *when* to worship.

Our heart is what matters in worshiping, not our voice. In other words, we can only worship God to the degree to which we know Him—the degree to which our heart is filled with love for Him. When we really know and love Him, it becomes easy and natural for us to worship. When we love other things *before* the Lord (or more than the Lord), then we'll end up serving two gods. (Exodus 20:3; Jeremiah 25:6) Anything that is more important to us than the Lord—money, other people, careers, status, beauty, sports, etc.—becomes another god.

It's interesting, because Scripture tells us that *we become like that which we worship*. My Chuck often uses the example of the Egyptians who worship the dung beetle. If you visit Egypt, you will notice the dung piles everywhere. It's a graphic illustration that we *do* become like that which we worship.

Consequently, our true relationship with God is expressed and shown in our worship of Him!

What Is the Purpose of Worship?

The goal and purpose of worship is to magnify, exalt, love and adore the only true God, Jesus Christ. In other words, *worship is simply a prayer of relationship in which the "created" lauds and magnifies the "Creator."* It's our expression of *His* worthiness. When we worship, we join the angels, the cherubim, the seraphim, the prophets, the apostles and the host of heaven falling down on their faces and exalting the one and only true God. Listen to Revelation 7:11-12, "And all the angels stood round about the throne, and *about* the elders and the four beasts, and fell before the throne on their faces, and worshiped God, saying, Amen! Blessing, and glory, and wisdom, and thanksgiving, and honor, and power, and might be unto our God forever and ever. Amen."

Seven further reasons *why* we worship are:

1) Worship is the primary reason behind all creation.
2) It's our realization of the holiness of God.
3) It's the prescribed ritual of the Temple in the Old Testament.
4) It's the proper response of a believer.
5) It's the recognition of our unworthiness before God.
6) It's the result of our fearing and reverencing God.
7) It's the manifestation of our relationship towards God and it's what makes everything else secondary.[2]

---

[2] David Hocking, *Hope for Today,* Tustin, California.

I truly believe that *if the body of Christ were really taught how to genuinely worship, it would revolutionize the Church!* Noah worshiped God, and as a result a brand new creation was born. (Genesis 6:9,18; 8:16-9:3) Abraham built an altar and worshiped the Lord and a whole nation resulted. (Genesis 12:7) Moses worshiped the Lord, and because of his obedience, God freed an entire people from the bondage of slavery. (Exodus 34:1-8) Men and women who truly learn to worship *can* change their world!

It's interesting to note that *prior* to Moses' revelation of God's glory on Mt. Sinai, he prayed, interceded, wept and pleaded with God, but he *never* worshiped. In other words, Exodus 34:8 is the first mention of him worshiping the Lord. This tells us that we too can pray, seek, weep, plead and call on the Lord, and yet never really worship. Look at me! (See Introduction.)

Even though the Lord is a Spirit, He still expresses emotion and is passionate. Thus, our worship can also be emotional and passionate as we express our love for Him. Worship is not simply an act of our willpower, but an all-consuming yearning in our spirit, as well as an overflowing of our emotions of gratitude and love. Throughout the Bible, you will see the prophets, the priests and the people of God unabashedly prostrating themselves and worshiping the Lord.

Consequently, worship involves all of our mental, emotional and spiritual facilities, *but the specific place we worship and express our love is in our spirit.* Remember John 4:23-24, "The hour cometh, and now is, when the *true worshipers shall worship the Father in spirit and in truth: for the Father seeketh such to worship Him. God is a Spirit: and they that worship Him must worship Him in spirit and in truth.*"

Thus, the purpose of worship is to adore, praise and love Him *in the same nature as He is—in the spirit.*

Faithful Is He Who Promised

Our external act of prostration simply denotes our inward attitude of humility and submission to His will. Worship communicates to the Lord that we are more concerned about *His Being* than *His gifts.* How often we confuse these two! We beseech the Lord for what He can give us, not simply for who He is. In other words, we worship and pray for *the gift*, not the Giver. I know I have certainly been guilty of this in the past.

Back in 1990, God gave me some incredible promises about future events in my life that would be mind-boggling. As I began to wait for these events to unfold, my eyes began to slip from a preoccupation with the *Giver* of the promise to the *promises* themselves. As I wearied myself through seven long years of waiting, God finally showed me my sin: *His promise had become more important than His Presence.* He began to teach me that real transformation can only occur when we learn to worship Him, occupied and satisfied with Him only, asking nothing in return.

An example we might all relate to is that of being loved by our children. One mother recently wrote me this precious account: "Nothing gives me more pleasure than to receive a kiss or a hug from my daughter *without my asking for one.* I love it when she extemporaneously takes me by the hand and wants me to be involved in whatever it is that she is doing."

It's the same thing with our Heavenly Father. Nothing brings Him more joy or pleasure than to receive a kiss or an expression of our adoration when He least expects it.

Our ability to worship Him does, however, depend upon our relationship to His promises. In other words, being assured that He will perform what He has spoken in His Word is absolutely essential. We must know that He will be faithful even amidst our greatest doubts and fears. In Romans 4:20, it is recorded that Abraham and Sara "...staggered not at the promise of God through unbelief, but were strong in faith, giving glory to God; and being fully persuaded that what He had promised, He was able also to perform." *They believed the promise because they believed the Promiser.* They *saw*, they *embraced* and they *received*, even though it took 13 long years for that promise to be fulfilled.

When God's promise seems to fail and the vision tarry, it's not a time to grow weary and give up, but a time to trust the Lord even more. Doubt is what robs us of our vision; faith is what allows us to unabashedly accept His promises, even though we cannot see or understand how they will ever come about. This was expressed in the life of Abraham "who against hope believed in hope." (Romans 4:18) The triumph of faith is seen just as much in the bearing of a temporary defeat, as it is in the securing of a victory. Overcomers are the ones who, in faith and love, find their way into the Holy Place and experience an intimacy with the Lord they never thought possible.

Fulness of Joy

How then is worship tied to joy?

The word *joy* actually means, "to brighten up, to rejoice or *to be happy.*" But the definition I find absolutely fascinating is from the root of the word joy, which means "to join." In other words, joy is the result of coming into God's presence, catching on fire with His Love and being joined or consumed in it. What this is saying is that *joy* only comes from being joined in spirit and worshiping Him. In other words, *joy is the result of the union and the communion of our spirits.*

"...I foresaw the Lord always before my face, for He is on my right hand, that I should not be moved: Therefore did my heart rejoice, and my tongue was glad; moreover also my flesh shall rest in hope:" ... "Thou hast made known to me the ways of life; Thou shalt make me full of joy with thy countenance." (Acts 2:25-26, 28)

Nehemiah 8:10 tells us that this joy is our strength. In other words, it's His joy that we receive when we become one with Him and this joy is what gives us our strength.   Proverbs 17:22 validates this when it says a merry [or joyful] heart makes us strong, but a broken spirit saps our strength.

If you search the Scriptures, you'll find the word *joy* ("the joy of our salvation") is often associated with *the Lord's presence* and with the offering of incense. Remember Psalm 16:11 which tells us, "Only *in His presence* is fulness of joy;" and other Scriptures like Psalm 51: 11-12: "Cast me not away from Thy presence...restore unto me the joy of Thy salvation." (See also Psalm 21:1; 43:4; Matthew 25:21; John 15:11; Jude 24.)

In other words, the kind of joy that we are talking about here—the joy of our salvation (or the "fulness of joy")—is a gift directly from God and comes only as a result of our being before His presence in worship. It comes from not only being overwhelmed with His Love and what He has done for us, but also from hearing His voice and knowing that He cares.

Worship, therefore, is not something we do just on Sundays and in church, but something we must learn to do every day. Look at the lives of Moses, Elijah, Samuel, Jeremiah, Daniel, Isaiah, John and Paul. These men didn't constrict their worship to just one day a week. They worshiped and loved the Lord continually, every day, all day long. And, as a result, Moses came to know the Lord "face to face" and was given incredible revelation (Exodus 33:11, 18); Isaiah was rewarded with incredible dreams and visions (Isaiah 25); and the glory of the Lord was certainly seen in the lives of Daniel, Elijah and Samuel.

The same can be true of us.

What is it then that keeps us from worshiping? Why wouldn't every believer want to experience the presence of the Lord like this? The first thing that comes to mind is that worship not only allows us to experience the Lord's revelation, joy and Love, but it also is the vehicle that God uses to expose more sin and self in us. Obviously, many Christians *do not* want to see this. Most of us know that more sin and self exists in us, but we think if we don't see it, then we don't have to deal with it. Those of us willing to risk exposure of these things, however, will enter His holy place and experience magnificent changes in our lives.

Another reason we don't worship as we should, is because of our misplaced priorities. Things like work, parenthood, ministry, busyness, etc., have become more important in our lives than sitting at the feet of Jesus. The Lord, of course, knows the real truth. We can fool each other, but He knows our hearts! Remember, He is seeking those who will worship Him, not only in spirit, *but in truth*!

The Key

The bottom line is that there's a proper order or procedure that we must follow in order to enter God's presence and worship Him. In other words, we cannot simply walk into His presence with unconfessed sin in our lives.

Debbie Holland, my precious sister in the Lord and partner in ministry, came up with a beautiful word picture that's appropriate here: We cannot go from the *covering* of the Lord to *communion* with the Lord, without first experiencing the *cleansing* of the Lord and the *consecration* of the Lord.

God is holy and thus, we can worship Him only when we, ourselves, are holy. Psalm 24:3-4 perfectly describes God's procedure for entering His presence: "Who shall ascend into the hill of the Lord? Or who shall stand in His holy place? *He who hath clean hands [or soul] and a pure heart [or spirit]....*" (See also Psalm 32:6)

The Lord is telling us here that the only ones permitted to worship Him are those with a cleansed soul and a purified spirit. Again, John 4:24, "God is a Spirit: and they that worship Him must worship Him in spirit and in truth." Worship is <u>not</u> some sort of ritual that we do *externally*, but a bowing down and a surrendering of ourselves *internally* —with our soul and spirit.

The story of Korah in the Old Testament dramatically portrays the importance God puts on properly entering His presence. (Numbers 16) Korah and 250 princes rose up against Moses and accused him of pride and of taking too much upon himself. Moses went to the Lord, sought His counsel and then powerfully spoke back to them, saying that God would show them the proper, required procedure for approaching Him: "Tomorrow the Lord will show who are His and who is holy..." He told them to take their censers, put fire and incense in them, and then put them before the Lord. He, then, would make it very apparent who was clean and who was not. Korah and his men did as Moses said. But Korah's incense was "strange incense" and "strange fire," meaning that it was <u>not</u>

prepared as God ordained. The Lord then appeared unto Moses and told him to "separate yourselves" from Korah and his congregation because He would "consume them." And it came to pass that the Lord did just that! The ground under Korah gave way, opened up, and swallowed him. Not only did he perish, but all his men and their houses also. The consequences of disobedience can be huge.

God means what He says and says what He means.

He makes the rules and our responsibility is not only to understand them, but also to apply them. 1 Chronicles 16:29 validates God's proper procedure for worshiping: "Give unto the Lord the glory due His Name; bring an offering and come before Him; *worship the Lord in the beauty of holiness.*" (Psalm 29:2) This Scripture tells us that in order to worship the Lord, we must *first* attain "the beauty of holiness."

The Beauty of Holiness

Worshiping "in the beauty of holiness" simply means *sin* has been dealt with and *self* has, for the moment, been set aside, so that Jesus' Life can come forth. In other words, it's Jesus' holiness that others see, not our own. Just as God's *Agape* Love is not our love and His supernatural Power, not our power, so this kind of holiness is <u>not</u> our holiness. Jesus is the only

One who is holy and He is the only One who makes holiness beautiful. Consequently, when we are clean and purified, the Lord is able to shine forth His holiness through us. In other words, we become "*partakers of His holiness.*" (Hebrews 12:10) We don't have to work at being holy, but simply relinquish ourselves and allow God to be holy through us. Holiness is simply the result of repentance and continuous sanctification. The soulish things in our lives have been cut away, and the spiritual things remain.

"According as He hath chosen us in Him before the foundation of the world, that *we should be holy and without blame before Him in love.*" (Ephesians 1:4)

This does not mean to say that "experientially" we will *always* stay in the beauty of holiness. Even though "positionally" this is an accomplished fact. The reality is that none of us can do this on a permanent basis! Romans 3:10 confirms this, "There is none righteous, no not one." Only Jesus was consistently holy. However, we can moment by moment go before the Lord, confessing and surrendering the things in our lives that are not of faith, and, then, be filled with the beauty of His holiness.

A holy person, consequently, is one who is not afraid of the light. In fact, he invites the light. He avows, "I want *all* the hidden things in my life to be revealed, because I want more of Jesus in me." He continually says, "Search me, O God, and know my heart; try me, and know my thoughts; And see if there be any wicked way in me, and lead me in the way everlasting." (Psalm 139:23-24)

A holy person is one who continually prays, "Let death work in me, so that [His] Life may be [seen and] received by others." (Paraphrase of 2 Corinthians 4:12) As God's people, we are to forsake all darkness and all secrecy and become open books read by all men. (2 Corinthians 3:2)

Leviticus 20:26 adjures us, "Ye shall be holy unto Me; for I, the Lord, am holy, and have severed you [sanctified]   from other people, that ye should be mine."

Worshiping Is Different Than Praising

Dr. R.A. Torrey, the great author and evangelist, testified that "transformation only came into [my] experience when [I] learned not only to give thanks [praise] to the Lord, but [also] to worship Him, asking nothing from Him, occupied and satisfied with Him alone."[3]

You see, worshiping the Lord is very different from simply praising Him. We praise God all day long—in

---

[3] *Intimacy with God,* page 21.

our car, at the office, at home, etc. However, we worship God only when we can truly enter His holy place, His presence. And, as we have seen, this only occurs when we are clean and holy. Another difference is that praise is often *seen*, whereas worship is secret— only God knows who the true worshipers are). Also, praise is one-way, whereas worship can be two-way (i.e., it often evokes a response from both parties). Next, praise is often horizontal in purpose, whereas worship is solely vertical. And finally, praise can sometimes be distant, whereas worship is always intimate.

A graphic example of the difference between praise and worship can be seen in the religious ceremonies that the priests of Solomon's Temple performed in the Old Testament. The priests praised the Lord when they *first* entered the Outer Courts of the Temple. There they raised their arms and hands straight up towards heaven, singing and praising the Lord as they proceeded through the outer gates. Worshiping the Lord, however, was something totally different. The priests worshiped God *last* and only in the Holy Place. In other words, they worshiped Him *after* they were cleansed, *after* they brought their incense offerings to the Golden Altar, and *after* they had prostrated themselves before the Incense Altar in the Holy Place.

This validates that as far as the priests were concerned, *worship was contingent upon their cleansing.* They could not go from the blood *covering* to *communion* without first going through *cleansing* and *consecration*. And the same thing holds true for us: we can only worship the Lord *after* we have given ourselves totally over to Him; and after we have received not only cleansed hands but also the purification of our spirit.

Remember Psalm 24:3-4, "Who shall ascend into the hill of the Lord? Or who shall stand in His Holy Place? *He who hath clean hands [or soul] and a pure heart [or spirit]...*"

Thus, if we adhere to the priestly pattern, the very *first thing* we are to do when we begin our prayer time with the Lord is to praise and thank Him. Scripture tells us that God "inhabits our praises" and this is exactly what we are imploring Him to do. The *final thing* we are supposed to do is to worship the Lord from our hearts. In other words, worship comes *after* we praise and *after* we are cleansed!

The bottom line is: we can only worship the Lord—we can only "catch fire"—when we have *already* gone through the steps of cleansing and we are *already* in the "beauty of His holiness." This is the point at which we truly become united, one in spirit and able to worship God as He desires.

God gave me a visual picture that might help to distinguish praise from worship. When we praise the

Lord our arms and hands are often outstretched towards heaven, symbolizing our adulation of the Lord. But when we worship Him, not only are our arms and hands outstretched towards heaven, our souls and spirits are also joined and intertwined with His, symbolizing our union, our oneness and our love relationship.

How About Us?

The question becomes, "How about us?"

How many of us fall down on our faces and worship the Lord daily in our prayer closets? *How many of us have caught fire with the Love of God and are being absolutely consumed by it?* How many of us are walking around exceedingly joyful (regardless of our circumstances) simply because we are in the presence of the Lord? Of course, we all pray, we all sing praises and on Sunday many of us raise our hands when we hear a moving song. But how many of us *really* come into His presence on a daily basis, prostrate ourselves (if not physically, at least our hearts), and truly worship Him? Of all the people I asked these very questions of, only one person said he did!

Jesus wants us to become so lost in our love for Him that we're able to experience His presence even in the midst of any difficult circumstances in which we find ourselves. Experiencing His presence is what will bring us unfathomable joy and what will restore the thrill of our salvation. The Lord wants us to be so *consumed* in the fire of His Love that we are able to withstand anything that He allows in our lives. We must be *passionately* in love with the Lord.

My Debbie looked up the word "passion" in Webster's Dictionary and what she found was surprising! The definition for passion is *extreme suffering.* Wow! In other words, those who are passionately in love with the Lord have learned to be so, by extreme suffering. Don't be frightened! In my book *Faith in the Night Seasons* I share that *suffering* simply means being "willing to set ourselves aside." This makes sense; those who are willing to relinquish themselves to the Lord will experience a passionate relationship with Him.

Without this kind of passion and without this kind of zeal, however, our love for the Lord can easily "grow cold" in the coming end times. (Matthew 24:12)

Remember Mary in the New Testament? She is a perfect example of one who truly worshiped the Lord. In Matthew 26:6-13, it says that she was so consumed in her love for Him that she didn't cease to kiss His feet, wash them with her tears and wipe them with her hair. Because of her display of love, Scripture tells us that she will be remembered throughout eternity. She set an example for all of us to follow—she single-mindedly worshiped the Lord *in spirit and in truth.*

We are told that Jesus said to Simon,"Seest thou this woman? I entered into thine house; thou gavest me no water for my feet. But she hath washed my feet with tears, and wiped them with the hair of her head. Thou gavest me no kiss. But this woman, since the time I came in, hath not ceased to kiss my feet. My head with oil thou didst not anoint. But this woman hath anointed my feet with ointment..." (Luke 7:44-46)

Chapter One
Questions

1) What is the *source* of our worship and what makes it a *two-way* communication?

   Spirit + Prayer

2) What does the word *worship* really mean? (Luke 7:45; 1 Corinthians 14:25)

3) Share some of your favorite Scriptures that demonstrate the definition of worship.

   John 4:23-24

4) One of the definitions of *worship* is "to catch fire." Why is this definition so appropriate?

   Really desire it, having a burning feeling, can't get enough of him.

5) "Worshiping in the spirit" means what? (John 4:23-24) Give a Scriptural example of a man or woman who did this. (Psalm 63:1-4; Matthew 26:6-13)

6) Why is *worship* so important? (Exodus 20:3; Job 14:17; Matthew 24:12) What is the purpose of *worship* and how is it perfected?

To keep in touch with the Lord + stay focused on him, not worshiping anyone or anything else but him.

7) Our ability to worship depends upon what? (Psalm 91 23:3-4; 1 Chronicles 16:29) What does the "beauty of holiness" really mean? (Hebrews 12:10; Leviticus 20:26)

Having faith in him, Cleansing, prayer, worship

8) What is the definition of *joy* and how is it tied to worship? (Psalms 16:11; 43:4; 51:11-12; Acts 2:28)

Brighten up + be happy joy is a result of coming into Gods presence.

9) What is it that keeps us from worshiping?

The worldly desires, priorities

10) How is worshiping the Lord different from simply praising Him? How is this validated in the temple model?

To worship him you have to be cleansed.

2

Pathway to Worship -
The Offering of Ourselves

Years ago, in one of David Wilkerson's[4] newsletters, there was an article entitled *The Making of a Man of God*. I've never forgotten that intriguing title because, in a nut shell, this is what God is trying to do in all of our lives—make us men and women of God.

If we really want to know *how* one becomes a "man of God," we have only to look at Jesus. He is our example. He is our role model. In other words, there is nothing that can happen to us that Jesus has not already experienced. Thus, to be made "like Him," we must face life-altering struggles similar to those He faced. Now obviously not to the same degree of intensity that Jesus did, but we too must come to the end of ourselves (death of self) so that we can learn to walk by His Spirit.

This means that, at some point in our walk with the Lord, we too will experience rejection, confusion and loneliness just as Jesus did. Each of these situations will provide us with a greater opportunity to die a little more to our self and to grow a little more in grace and the image of God.

---

[4] Pastor of Times Square Church in New York City..

John 12:24 validates this principle: "Verily, verily I say unto you, Except a corn of wheat fall into the ground and die, it abideth alone: but if it die, it bringeth forth much fruit."

Total surrender and relinquishment seems to be the *cost* of "going all the way with God."

Psalm 34:19 tells us that, "Many are the afflictions of the righteous," but if we yield ourselves to the Lord, He promises to deliver us out of all of them. Now, it's not our job to *understand all* that He is doing, but simply to surrender everything and *trust Him in all* that He is doing.

Surrender Is Key

David Wilkerson defines the term *surrender* as "giving up or relinquishing something to another that is granted to you." To me, this is a perfect definition. When God calls us to surrender *all* to Him, He is simply asking us to give back to Him the life that He granted us in the first place. In other words, we're not being forced to lay our lives down, it's a choice that we are making out of our own free will and out of our love for Him.

When all is said and done, I truly believe we won't only be judged by *what we did for Him*, but by *how much we surrendered to Him,* how much we loved Him and how much our hearts and lives were totally yielded to Him.

Love Vs. Worship

As we said last chapter, worship flows from love. The word used in Scripture for the verb "to love" is the Greek word *agapao,* which means "to totally give oneself over to something." Love for God, then, is not just an emotional *feeling* but a complete surrender of ourselves, heart, mind and soul. Consequently, when we don't know how to love God—how to completely surrender our lives to Him—we will never be able to truly worship Him. Love comes before worship. Without Love we can't worship. Therefore, we must learn how to love the Lord *before* we can learn to really worship Him.

We must love Christ (totally give ourselves over to Him) in order to become "cleansed," in order to experience the "beauty of *His* holiness," and in order to worship Him. As we saw in the last chapter, being in the beauty of His holiness is the requirement for entering His presence. It's also the requirement for staying there. We not only must have the boldness, the cleanliness and the purity to enter His holy place, we must also have the beauty of His holiness in order to remain there.

As we said, Jesus is our example and His walk our blueprint. There are two evidences that Jesus loved the

Father and was totally surrendered to Him. First, He was completely obedient to His will. Second, He experienced the manifestation of His Father's presence continually.

In order for us to prove that we love Jesus, we too must walk in complete obedience to His will. We must learn not only *how* to make faith choices to do His will, regardless of how we feel or what we think, but also how to become cleansed vessels so that we, too, can experience His presence.

The only other choice we have is to succumb to our difficult circumstances, trials and tribulations. This, of course, will quench His Spirit in us and cause us to walk by the flesh. Our job, again, is not to necessarily understand all that God allows in our lives but simply to trust Him *in* all that He allows.

In summary, we can only worship the Lord to the degree that we love Him—the degree to which we are surrendered, cleansed and holy.

The Temple Revisited

Speaking of being surrendered, cleansed and holy, let's turn back, for just a moment, to the cleansing ceremony that the Lord ordained for the priests of Solomon's Temple.

Years ago, when I wrote my first book *The Way of Agape*, the Lord led me to make a thorough exploration of the Temple of Solomon. I was fascinated by the similarities between the architecture of that temple and that of our own internal architectural design. While in Jerusalem on one of our trips, I was able to spend some quality time in the Rockefeller Museum, gathering as much information on this subject as I could. Several rabbis studying in the library at the same time, were delighted to help me with the project. They were so touched that a "goyim" (a gentile) was interested in their sacred temple that they brought me as many books as they could find written in English.

One of the reasons that this temple fascinated me so much was that there are over 52 chapters in the Bible that refer to this temple and its services in some way. In God's economy, I figured this *must* have some importance. If He dedicated that much space to this topic, He must be saying something extremely significant. Besides, Solomon's Temple was unique. It was the only temple of the three (Solomon's, Nehemiah's and Herod's) in which the Spirit of God—the Shekinah Glory—permanently dwelt in the Holy of Holies. (Exodus 25:22) In later temples, God's presence seemed to come and go. Also, Solomon's Temple was the only temple in which God gave King David precise directions for its construction and also for all its furnishings. (1 Chronicles 28:12 and 19) And, finally, Solomon's Temple was the only temple in which the Ark of the Covenant rested. By the time the other temples were built, it had disappeared. Solomon's Temple lasted for 410 years until it was finally destroyed by King Nebuchadnezzar.[5]

As I began to explore the intricacies of this fascinating temple—the Holy of Holies, the Holy Place, the Inner and Outer Courts—I began to see many parallels between its blueprint and the interior architecture of man (i.e. spirit, heart, soul and body).

For example, the hallmark of Solomon's Temple were the pillars that stood in front of the sanctuary called Jachin and Boaz. My first question to the Lord was: "Why did these pillars have names at all and why on earth, the names Jachin and Boaz?" These pillars weren't functional; they were simply there for show. So, why did God name them Jachin and Boaz? In the Old Testament, Boaz lived during the period of the Judges, around 1200 B.C. (See the book of Ruth.) Solomon's Temple wasn't even constructed until 200-300 years later in the era of David and his son, Solomon. So, again, why the name Boaz?

Jachin means "in His Counsel" and Boaz means "by His Strength."

When I was studying and writing my book *Be Ye Transformed*, the Lord validated over and over again the

<hr>

[5] See picture of temple on pages 34-35 in *The Light of the Temple* book.

Diagram 1: Solomon's Temple

incredible comparison, not only between the floorplan of Solomon's Temple and the interior architecture of man, but also between the features and furniture of that temple and the components that make up the Mind of Christ in us. In 1 Corinthians 3:16 it says, "Know ye not that ye are the temple of God, and that the Spirit of God dwelleth in you?"

If you line up the features of the Mind of Christ as listed in Isaiah 11—the Spirit of the Lord, the Spirit of wisdom and understanding, *the spirit of counsel and strength,* and the spirit of knowledge and fear of the Lord—with the physical furniture and features of the temple, *the two pillars, Jachin (which means <u>counsel</u>) and Boaz (which means <u>strength</u>), align perfectly with the spirit of counsel and strength.* All the other components of the Mind of Christ also line up perfectly with their corresponding feature of the temple. (If you are interested in further details, check out Chapter 13 in *Be Ye Transformed.*)

Is this just a coincidence? I don't think so! To me, it validates the handprint of God and the divine connection between the architecture of man and Solomon's Temple.[6]

Thus, there are important principles that we can glean from studying Solomon's Temple and the ceremonies that God ordained there for worship. The Lord tells us that everything in the Bible, from the of

---

[6] See *Be Ye Transformed* for more details.

smallest detail to the greatest, is there for our learn-ing. (Romans 15:4) In other words, He has given us many visual pictures throughout the Bible to help us understand His ways a little more clearly. Solomon's Temple is definitely one of these.

The Order of Worship in Solomon's Temple

So how did the priests in this temple worship the Lord? What was their order of service like?

See Chart 1: The Temple Blueprint (on the next page).

Let me first give you an "overall picture" and then we'll come back and explore each area of service in greater detail. The order of service for the priests was as follows:

After the Levites opened the <u>Outer Court</u> gate for the people, they began to sing and praise the Lord. Then, the priests entered the <u>Inner Court</u> and imme-diately went to the Lavers of Bronze where they washed their hands and feet. After that they approached the Brazen Altar (or Holocaust Altar), where they sacrificed their animals in order to purge the sins of the people. Next, they immersed themselves bodily in the Molten Sea. And, finally, they took a censer full of hot coals from the Brazen Altar, went back into the <u>Holy Place</u> where they changed their clothes, took some incense and sprinkled it over the coals at the Golden Incense Altar where God promised to "meet with them." (Exo-dus 25:22) Approaching the Golden Altar of

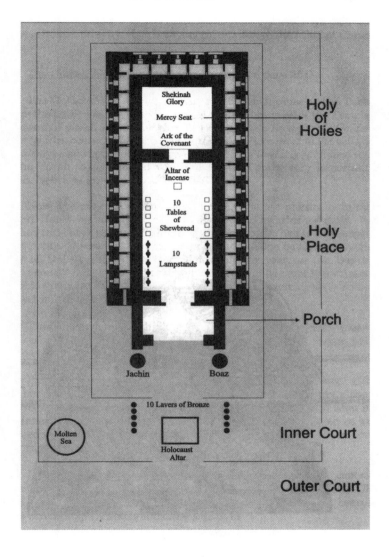

Diagram 2: Blueprint of Interior of Solomon's Temple

Incense, they took off their shoes, prostrated themselves and worshiped the Lord in the "beauty of holiness."

"Give unto the Lord the glory due unto His name; bring an offering, and come before Him; worship the Lord in the *beauty of holiness*." (1 Chronicles 16:29)

"Give unto the Lord the glory due unto His name; worship the Lord in the *beauty of holiness*." (Psalm 29:2)

"Oh, worship the Lord in the *beauty of holiness*; fear before Him, all the earth." (Psalm 96:9)

Upon leaving the Holy Place, the priests then shared of the fullness of the Lord (or the anointing) that they had received at the Golden Altar by addressing all the people who had gathered in the courtyard. One of the passages they recited was Numbers 6:24-26: "The Lord bless thee, and keep thee; the Lord make His face shine upon thee, and be gracious unto thee; the Lord lift up His countenance upon thee, and give thee peace." They repeated this entire ceremony twice a day, once in the morning and once at night.

The Outer Court

Now, let's explore each of these courtyards and each of these ceremonies in a little more detail.

---

[7] *The Holy Temple of Jerusalem,* Chaim Richman, page 95.

All of Israel had access to the Outer Courts and, thus, could freely come in and out. Whereas, only the priests could enter into the holy sanctuary.

The first thing that occurred in the Outer Court was that the trumpets were sounded and the Levites opened the gates for the people to enter. Psalm 118:19-23 describes this scene: "Open to me the gates of righteousness…" These are the gates that lead to the presence of the Lord. Other Levite priests ascended the platform that faced the outer altar and they, too, began to sing.

"O come, let us sing unto the LORD: let us make a joyful noise to the rock of our salvation. Let us come before His presence with thanksgiving, and make a joyful noise unto Him with psalms." (Psalm 95:1-2; see also Psalms 100:2 & 4; 118:19.)

The Levites were commissioned not only to guard all the temple gates, but also to sing a new song each day. Sunday they sang Psalm 24; Monday, Psalm 48; Tuesday, Psalm 82; Wednesday, Psalm 94; Thursday, Psalm 81; Friday, Psalm 93; and Saturday, Psalm 92.[7] These songs were as important to the service as were the priestly duties themselves. Three times during their song, they would pause while the priests sounded their silver trumpets and all the people in the courtyard would fall down and prostrate themselves before the

Diagram 3: Levites Singing in Outer Court

Lord. They did this both at the beginning and at the end of the service.

The Inner Court

The official priests—only those who were a direct descendant of Aaron—would then enter the Inner Courtyard, wash their hands and feet at the *Lavers of Bronze* and await the time for the slaughtering of the sacrifices.

When the time arrived, the priests moved to the *Brazen Altar* where they sacrificed their offerings in order to symbolically remove the sins of the people in order that they could be reconciled to God. Finally, the priests bathed in the *Molten Sea* by complete bodily immersion as a symbol that God had, indeed, washed away their sins. Thus, the Inner Court was known as the cleansing and atoning area.

The Holy Place

Fire, incense, tapestry and gold all led the priest higher and higher up to the Holy Place and the Incense Altar where he worshiped the Lord.

Following the offering of the sacrifices in the Inner Court, one of the priests gathered some hot coals in a brass carrier from the Brazen Altar and carried them

Diagram 4: The Outer and Inner Courts

into the Holy Place, where he promptly changed his clothes. Once he had "put off" his dirty clothes and "put on" his clean ones, he picked up the hot coals and placed them on the Incense Altar. Another priest stood by, holding the incense. A third priest took the incense in the palms of his hands and after the first two left, scattered the incense over the hot coals. The fire and the smoke from the incense rose up toward the ceiling, spread out and filled the entire sanctuary. (1 Kings 8:10-11)

The last priest then prostrated himself on the ground. While all this was going on, the other priests came to the Holy Place to witness the offering of incense and they, too, prostrated themselves.

Upon leaving the temple sanctuary, the head priest stood upon the steps facing the congregation in the Outer Court. The rest of the priests joined him there and they all extended their hands towards heaven and called upon the unutterable Name of God. The head priest then blessed the people and recited Scriptures. At this reading, the rest of the priests and all the people again fell on their faces and worshiped God.

It's interesting to note how often during these services, the priests prostrated themselves and worshiped God. At the end of the service, the Levites readied themselves for their final choir duties.

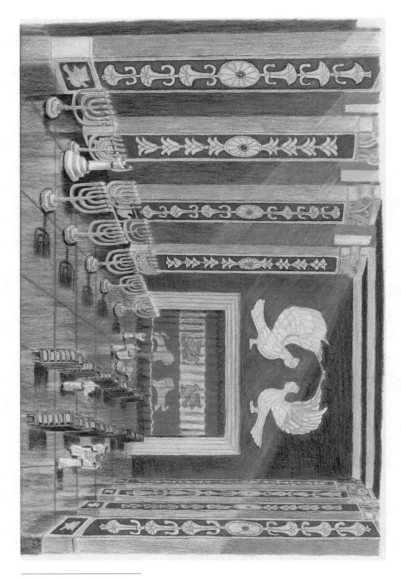

Diagram 5: The Holy Place

Scripture was again read and prayers were given. This same worship service was performed twice a day, morning and evening.

It's interesting to note: All of Israel had access to the Outer Courts of Solomon's Temple, but only the sanctified priests had access to the Incense Altar in the Holy Place. Also note, *the priests dealt with their sin and were reconciled to God in the Inner Court, but they worshiped Him and said their prayers before His presence in the Holy Place.* In addition, the coals from the Brazen Altar in the Inner Court were the same coals used to light the Altar of Incense in the Holy Place. Any other fire was called "strange fire" because it was not used as God designed. (Again, remember the story of Korah in Numbers 16.)

The Golden Altar—also known as "the Altar before the Lord"—was considered in God's eyes to be the most sacred part of the temple. The incense offering there was noted to be the most acceptable because it expressed God's divine mercy and His benevolence. (Exodus 30:10) Note: in Leviticus 16:12-13, Hebrews 9:3 and Revelation 8:3, it speaks about the golden censer (the Incense Altar) being "within the veil in the Holiest of all." There is a hint here that even though the Golden Incense Altar sat in the Holy Place just in front of the veil, it was always considered to be a part of (or connected to) the Holy of Holies (the "holiest"). Officiating at this Altar happened only once

---

[8] See Passover Service in the *Light of the Temple* book.

Diagram 6: All of Israel Coming to the Temple

in each priest's life, so he had to be fully prepared to do everything perfectly.[8] (Leviticus 4:7, 18; 16:18)

How Does All of This Apply to Us?

Question: Does this Jewish, Old Testament, Old Covenant temple service have anything at all to do with us gentile, New Testament, New Covenant believers? In other words, can we apply what we have learned here to our own daily, devotional times? Yes, it seems we can.

I am fully aware that we are *not* under the Law nor under the Old Covenant, but under grace and the New Covenant. (Romans 6:14) So, I do *not* mean to imply that there's some sort of ritual or ceremony that we must do in order to work our way towards God. That's not what I am saying at all. However, I do believe that by this service God has given us a "set of guidelines" and that by following these suggestions not only will our devotional times be acceptable to Him, but also they will become an incredible blessing to us. The most important thing we, as New Testament believers, can do is allow the Holy Spirit the freedom to direct us. Because, of course, only He knows the "perfect" way for us to worship.

Again, God made the rules; we must simply carry them out. However, in order to carry them out, we must first understand what they are.

Let's briefly explore what the Word of God has to say about worshiping and see if there is any connection to Solomon's Temple and its priests. A couple of obvious Scriptural connections are 1 Corinthians 3:16 and 2 Corinthians 6:16, which both tell us that "we are the temple of God" and that the "Spirit of God dwells in us," just as He did in Solomon's Temple. Paul is making an analogy or a word picture here by saying that our body is a temple and the Holy Spirit dwells in us. Remember that in the Old Testament the Holy Spirit dwelt in the Holy of Holies of Solomon's Temple. Scripture tells us that now God's Spirit dwells in "temples not made with hands"—i.e., us. (Acts 17:24)

1 Peter 2:9 also tells us that: "[We] are...a royal priesthood...that should show forth the praises of Him who hath called [us] out of darkness into His marvelous light." And verse 5 of that same chapter says, "...[We] also, ...a holy priesthood, [should] offer up spiritual sacrifices, acceptable to God by Jesus Christ."

And, there is Revelation 1:6 which says, "Jesus Christ hath made us kings and *priests* unto God..." And, Revelation 5:10 which says, "He hath made us kings and priests that we should reign upon the earth." And, finally, Hebrews 10:19-24 and Revelation 5:8 talk about New Testament saints having "boldness to enter the holiest and worship."

Psalm 27:4 validates all of the above: "One thing have I desired of the Lord, that will I seek after; that I may dwell in the house of the Lord all the days of my life, to behold the beauty of the Lord, and to inquire in His temple."

Thus, there seems to be a valid Scriptural comparison between the true worshiper of God who "worships the Lord in spirit and truth," (John 4:23), and the priests of Solomon's Temple who worshiped the Lord "in the beauty of holiness" at the Incense Altar. Again, the former was under the Old Covenant without Christ, and the latter, under the New Covenant with Christ. But, the comparison is there and Scripture seems to suggest that it is important.

How does God want us to apply this priestly worship service to our own lives? How do we go about entering the Lord's presence? What is the practical application for all of this?

Let's continue on...

Chapter Two
Questions

1) How does one truly become "Christ-like"? How is Jesus our role model in this process? (John 12:24) What were the two evidences in His life that proved He was totally surrendered to the Father?

2) What seems to be the "cost" of going all the way with the Lord? What's the *key*? (1 Corinthians 4:12-13) In the end, what will we be judged on?

3) What does the term "to love" really mean? Explain how this affects our worshiping the Lord?

4) How can we prove that we love Jesus? (Matthew 22:37-39)

5) We can only worship the Lord to the degree that we are _____, _____ and _____.

6) What was it about Solomon's Temple that made it so different from the others? (Exodus 25:22; 1 Chronicles 28:12, 19)

7) What were the three pieces of furniture in the Inner Court of that temple that the priests ministered at?

8) Where was it that the priests of Solomon's Temple worshiped? Why was this room or this place so unique?

9) Where did the *Altar of Incense* actually sit in Solomon's Temple? Where does Hebrews 9:3-5 and Leviticus 16:12-13 seem to imply that it sat?

10) Do you see a valid Scriptural connection between the true worshiper of God and the priests of Solomon's Temple?

Preparation for Worship - Personal Surrender

Clean Hands and a Pure Heart

There is an old proverb that says, "We only prepare for what we think is important." And, it's so true. If we don't feel that the subject at hand is important, then we certainly won't prepare for it. However, if the issue is something that matters greatly to us, then we'll conscientiously do whatever is necessary to make ready for it.

The same principle applies when we want to enter the Lord's presence. Read Psalm 24:3-4 again with this preparation in mind: "Who shall ascend into the hill of the Lord? Or who shall stand in His *holy place*? He that hath *clean hands*, and *a pure heart*; who hath not lifted up his soul unto vanity, nor sworn deceitfully. He shall receive the blessing from the Lord, and righteousness from the God of his salvation."

James 4:8 expresses the same principle: "Draw near to God and He will draw near to you. *Cleanse your hands*...and *purify your hearts*..."

These Scriptures tells us that the only path to the Holy Place is by having clean hands and a pure heart—

i.e., being in the beauty of *His* holiness. By continually confessing and repenting of anything that is not of faith, the Lord cleanses our soul (*clean hands*) and gives us a *pure heart*. Scripture says that these two things are the only ticket inward! Remember Psalm 66:18, which tells us that "if we regard iniquity in our heart, the Lord will not hear us."

The reason He can't hear us is because sin separates, destroys, corrupts, divides, robs, perverts, damages, distorts, blinds, weakens, ruins and kills. If not addressed, sin can become an obstacle, a barrier and a wall between us and prevent our fellowship. Now, we won't lose our salvation when this happens but our communication with the Lord will be affected. Therefore, repentance—the desire to turn around and follow God—is the key to holiness. It's what allows us to truly worship the Lord in spirit and truth. True repentance awakens a hatred of sin in our lives and results in a genuine fear of the Lord. Consequently, only confession and repentance will give us a clean heart, a renewed spirit and restored fellowship.

Thus, a person who is holy is simply one who is totally surrendered to God. (Exodus 40:15; Deuteronomy 18:5; Leviticus 21:6-8) Holiness simply means "one who is *set apart unto God's service*. It does not mean continual purity (only Jesus could maintain this), but a constant recognition of one's sin and the choice to deal with it.

If the priests did not wash their hands and feet in the lavers before they worshiped, or if they tried to offer "strange" incense (as we saw in the case of Korah), God would make their "inward condition" very visible. Either they would contact leprosy or, like Korah, they would be killed. In like manner, if we try to worship the Lord *before* becoming clean, *before* having a renewed spirit, *before* putting on the beauty of His holiness, God's Spirit will be quenched and our worship polluted.

Holiness has everything in the world to do with our proximity to the throne.

Worship is the highest expression of our love for God. It's simply the paring down of our motives to "love" alone. Only love and holiness have access to the Lord's presence. Holiness means being cleansed enough to love God with all our heart, mind and soul and a vessel of His Love to others. Just as the priests reflected God's glory when they came forth from the Holy Place, we too should reflect the Lord's holiness after we have been with Him.

Fear of God

Therefore, until we are holy, we will be unable to "see" the Lord. Hebrews 12:14 confirms this: "Follow …holiness, without which no man will see the Lord." Simply having the Word of God in our laps does not make us holy; nor does scholarship, without application, sanctify us. *The only real test of whether or not we are holy, is if we walk in progressive freedom from sin and self.* The Bible calls this the "fear of the Lord."

"Fear of the Lord" means essentially two things: 1) To stand in reverential awe of who God is and 2) to hate sin. These two principles are irrevocably linked. In other words, we can't stand reverentially in awe of who God is until we really *know* Him and have an intimate relationship with Him. And we can't know Him unless we *hate sin*—i.e., flee anything that quenches His Life in us. So, *knowing God intimately* and *walking in the fear of Him* must go hand in hand.

"My son, if thou wilt receive My words, and hide My commandments with thee; so that thou incline thine ear unto wisdom, and apply thine heart to understanding; yea, if thou criest after knowledge, and liftest up thy voice for understanding; if thou seekest her as silver, and searchest for her as for hid treasures; then shalt thou understand the Fear of the Lord, and find the Knowledge of God." (Proverbs 2:1-5)

"Fear of God" does not mean fearfulness of God or being afraid of Him, but walking, speaking and acting in such an intimate relationship with Him that we are in continual awe of what He is doing in our life. And because of this intimacy, we are constantly watching for and fleeing anything that would hinder or quench it.

"Fear of God" is caring more about what God thinks than about what we think.

Consequently, in order to worship the Lord as He desires, we must first become free from sin, even if it's only for a few minutes. "Draw nigh to God, and He will draw nigh to you. *Cleanse your hands...and purify your hearts...."* (James 4:8)

Personal Application

How is this personal cleansing process accomplished? What must we do in order to surrender ourselves completely to the Lord? Can we just yield ourselves to the Lord once in the morning and stay cleansed all day long, or is more required?

Jesus tells us that everything in His Word is there for our learning, our understanding, and for us to apply to our lives. Here again, we can gain more understanding of what God desires by exploring the priest's worship services in Solomon's Temple. This worship service, to me, is the model or the pattern that the Lord had laid out for us in Scripture in order to deal with our sin, be reconciled to God and allowed to enter His presence. What specifically were the priests required to do?

If you remember, upon entering the Inner Court, the priests encountered three pieces of furniture—*the*

Lavers, where the priests washed their hands and feet (Exodus 30:19-21); *the Brazen Altar* where they gave their sin offerings to the Lord; and, *the Molten Sea* where they bathed bodily. These are the same three cleansing steps that God wants us to implement in order to wash ourselves from "the filthiness of [our] flesh and spirit" and be enabled to enter His presence.

"Having therefore these promises, dearly beloved, let us cleanse ourselves from all *filthiness of the flesh and spirit,* perfecting holiness in the fear of God." (2 Corinthians 7:1) See also Psalm 15:1-2.

Thus, what we are about to learn is not something I've made up or something I read in a self-help psychology book, but the actual steps that the priests took in order to approach the Holy Place and worship the Lord. Following these steps will allow us not only to deal with our sin and self, but also to worship Him as He desires.

We Must Be Believers

First of all, it's very important to understand that unless we have asked Jesus into our hearts to be our Savior and have been *born again* by His Spirit, these steps will <u>not</u> work. In other words, in order for this cleansing process to work, we must *first* have a brand-new spirit (or power source or life source) within us that *will* produce something different than what we naturally think, feel and want to do. John 3:5-6 validates this: "...Except a man be born of water and of the Spirit, he cannot enter into the kingdom of God. That which is born of the flesh is flesh; and that which is born of the Spirit is spirit."

Non-believers can always make a choice, but none of them have the *authority* or the *power* to go against how they really feel or what they really think, because they don't possess a supernatural power within them (God's Spirit) to perform anything different. Believers, indwelt by the Holy Spirit, do!

A Christian, one who has Christ dwelling in his heart, has *God's* authority and *God's* power to override his negative thoughts and feelings and say, "not my will, but Thine." (Matthew 26:39) God, then, in His timing and in His way, will not only align his feelings with what he has chosen by faith, but also give him the power to do God's will in his life.

Putting Off our Sin and Putting On Christ

Therefore, not only must we be believers in order to enter God's presence, but we must also be clean. In other words, we cannot just walk into the Holy Place any time we feel like it. God is holy and will commune only with those who are holy. He cannot abide where there is corruption, sin or self. Consequently, in order to worship Him as He desires, we must first *put off* any sin and self and *put on* Christ.

Over and over again throughout Scripture we are exhorted to *put off* the flesh and to *put on* Christ. (Ephesians 4:22-24; Colossians 3:8-10) Thus, the practical application of just how we do this, can be patterned after the three steps that the priests took in the Inner Court of Solomon's Temple in order to deal with their sin and be reconciled to God.

Listen to Psalm 51, "Wash me thoroughly from mine iniquity, and cleanse me from my sin. For I acknowledge my transgressions: and my sin is ever before me."... "Purge me with hyssop, and I shall be clean: wash me, and I shall be whiter than snow"... "Create in me a clean heart, O God: and renew a right spirit within me." (verses 2, 3, 7 and 10)

Personal Cleansing Steps

The following, then, are a brief overview of the specific cleansing steps to putting off our sin and self and to putting on Christ. (If you want an in-depth explanation of how these essential steps can change your life, I would really recommend taking a look at our book *The Key*.)

(Note: there were really only three steps that the priests took, but because so much happens in the first step, for simplicity's sake I have divided it into two separate parts.)

1) The first essential step we must take in order to be a cleansed vessel, is to <u>recognize and acknowledge the negative thoughts and emotions</u>—the self-life—that has just occurred. We want to "take our thoughts captive," look at them and allow God to give us His insight. We're not to *vent* these things nor *push them down* into the hidden part of our soul, but simply ask the Lord to expose what's *really* going on inside us.

This is what the priests did at the Lavers of Bronze. The lavers themselves were made of a woman's looking glass (mirrors of polished metal). As the priests bent over the lavers to wash their hands, what they actually saw was their own reflection (their own true self) in the mirrored lavers.

The priest's actions are symbolic of what the Lord requires us to do. We are to ask Him not only to expose what's going on in our surface *(conscious)* thoughts and emotions—things that we can see, but also to shed light on the *hidden things* in our soul—the things we cannot see.

Our surface emotions can often be just the *symptoms* of a much deeper cause. If the real root problem can be exposed, and subsequently gotten rid of, then the surface emotions will not occur again either. If we only deal with the external emotions, however, and never the root cause, the surface problems will come back and back and back. Therefore, it's essential that we always ask the Lord to expose any root cause.

Now, whenever I find myself hurt, angry, resentful, envious, critical, self-centered, prideful, ungrateful, anxious, afraid, confused, bitter, judgmental or filled with any ungodly emotion, I try to stop and get alone with the Lord so I can go through these steps. Jesus is the only One who can expose and cleanse my sin. And, thus, He's the only One who can really heal me.

Often, as the insight comes, the tears will flow. Bob Sorge, in his wonderful book *Secrets of the Secret Place*, says that "tears are liquid words." How profound and true that is. Tears often express what I, in words, cannot.

2) The second essential step of the Inner Court ritual is to now <u>confess and repent of all that the Holy Spirit has shown us</u> and, in addition, <u>unconditionally forgive</u> anyone who has wronged us.

Confession simply means "owning" our negative thoughts, emotions and actions and acknowledging that what we have done, either ignorantly or knowingly, has quenched God's Spirit in us. Because it's sin, we must, therefore, confess "ownership" of it.

Repenting is choosing to turn around from following what our negative thoughts and emotions are telling us and, instead, choosing to follow what God wants.

This critical step of confession and repentance is our *own responsibility.* As 1 John 1:9 says, "If *we* confess our sins, [then] *He* is faithful and just to forgive us our sins..."

This is the step, however, that many of us leave out when we give things to the Lord. Certainly, we've relinquished our hurts, fears and doubts to God, but often we've forgotten to admit our own responsibility in the situation. And this is why so many of the things we've given to God, often come back. If we *don't* do our part by confessing and repenting of our sin, God is hindered from doing His—taking our sins away "as far as the east is from the west." (Psalm 103:12)

"I acknowledged my sin unto Thee, and mine iniquity have I not hid...I will confess my transgressions unto the Lord; and Thou forgavest the iniquity of my sin." (Psalm 32:5)

A part of this second step is that we must also **unconditionally forgive** others for whatever ill they have done to us. Unforgiveness is one of the many things that quenches God's Spirit in us. And, if we hold on to that unforgiveness, it will hinder God from working *in* us and *through* us. Therefore, the way we release God to work in our situations is by unconditionally forgiving the other party, whether or not they have asked for it!

"For if ye forgive men their trespasses, your heavenly Father will also forgive you: But if ye forgive not men their trespasses, neither will your Father forgive your trespasses." (Matthew 6:14-15)

Now, don't misunderstand me, we are not pardoning these people. We don't have the authority to do that. That's God's responsibility. When we unconditionally forgive them, we are simply releasing them to God, so that He can then judge them righteously, and so that our response to their sin won't become a stumbling block in us.

(Both of the above steps occur at the Lavers of Bronze.)

3) Once God has revealed our ungodly thoughts and emotions and we have confessed our responsibility in them, the next essential step is to give everything that the Lord has shown us, that is not of faith, over to Him. God will not violate our free will by forcibly taking

these things from us; we must willingly sacrifice or choose to hand them over.

We are told in Romans 12:1 that we must present our bodies to the Lord as a "living sacrifice." In other words, God wants us to give Him—to sacrifice to Him—everything that is not of faith, so that it can be purged and cleansed by His Blood. As we willingly give

Him our sin, He promises to take it, "As far as the east is from the west...." (Psalm 103:12)

This is exactly what the priests did at the Brazen Altar as they sacrificed their offerings to the Lord. 2 Chronicles 7:1 gives us a vivid picture of just what happened: "Now when Solomon had ceased praying, the fire came down from heaven and consumed the burnt offering [i.e., absorbed it on the Brazen Altar] and the sacrifices; and the glory of the Lord filled the house."

(It's interesting because Isaiah 4:4 tells us that in the "end times" the remnant church will again be purged and brought through her trials by *God's consuming fire* and then, filled with His glory.)

Psalm 51:17 explains that "the sacrifices of God are a broken spirit; [and] a broken and a contrite heart..." These things He will "not despise."

We can also offer God the sacrifice of *praise* (Hebrews 13:15; Jeremiah 33:11); the sacrifice of *righteousness* (Psalm 4:5); the sacrifice of *joy* (Psalm 27:6); and the sacrifice of *thanksgiving.* (Psalm 116:17; 107:22) These are all defined as "sacrifices," because, during our trials and troubles, we certainly don't "feel" like praising Him, being thankful or joyful. But, as we choose to do it anyway, He will be faithful to align our feelings with the faith choices we have made and make us genuine.

Being a living sacrifice means offering God the best of what we have to offer—ourselves! His Word tells us that offerings like this rise to Him as sweet smelling savor. This sweet savor was the difference between Cain and Abel's offering. Abel followed God's instructions and his sweet smelling sacrifice was accepted. Cain, on the other hand, did not obey God's prescribed order and, thus, his offering was rejected because it had no sweet aroma. In other words, there was no connection, no exchange and no purpose achieved in Cain's offering. The same principle applies to us.

Now, most of the things that we give to the Lord are "of the flesh" and, usually, will go away immediately or at least within a few days, if we are faithful to go through these four cleansing steps. However, some of the things that the Lord might expose will be long-standing strongholds of the enemy. And he won't let these things go easily. So don't be dismayed if certain thoughts and feelings seem to reappear even after you have given them to God.

The truth is that the Lord takes our self-life the moment we give it to Him, but often *our feelings don't align with those choices for awhile.* And this is where Satan tries to make us think that God is not faithful and that He has not taken our sins away. Satan wants to use these "in-between" times—between the time we give ourselves to God and the time the Lord finally aligns our feelings with our choices—to try to destroy us. <u>God</u>, on the other hand, lets us go as long as He knows is wise, to test us and to strengthen our faith. The question He is constantly asking us is: "Will you trust Me? Will you trust Me in spite of what you see, think or feel?"

Another important reminder is that we must be cleansed in order to respond the way God would have us. In other words, never take a stand with someone or confront someone unless you are a cleansed vessel. If you are not clean, it will be "flesh" out there, not the "spirit" at all, and the encounter will go poorly. Believe me, I know. I've tried it a hundred times the wrong way and it doesn't work! *Self, no matter how polished it is, does not accomplish anything!* The other party will immediately sense our judgmental attitude, react from his defenses, the truth will be hidden and we'll sink even deeper into the pit than we were before.

If we can get clean first, then we can respond from God's Love and His Wisdom; the other person will sense our unconditional acceptance, respond from his heart and the situation will have a chance to turn around.

4) The fourth essential step in dealing with our sin and self is that after we have sacrificed everything to the Lord, we must <u>read His Word</u> and replace any lies with His Truth. God is the only One who can *cleanse, sanctify and heal our souls* completely by His Word.

Remember, it was at the Molten Sea—a huge bathtub that held 2000 baths—that the priests immersed themselves bodily in order to receive a total cleansing. They had gotten all "blood splattered" at the Brazen Altar where they sacrificed their offerings. Now they needed a complete bodily bathing in order to be thoroughly cleansed.

In like manner, after we have confessed, repented and sacrificed all to the Lord, we, too, are "bloody" and "torn apart" and in desperate need of God's complete healing power. Only reading or reciting Scriptures from the Word of God, can totally restore us at this point. In other words, only the Lord can wash us "with the washing of water by the Word." (Ephesians 5:26)

It's very helpful to memorize appropriate Scriptures, so that if we are away from our Bibles, we can still put the Word of God back down in our innermost part where the lies have been. Scriptures like:

"I [have] acknowledged my sin unto Thee, and mine iniquity have I not hid... I [have] confessed my transgressions unto the Lord; and Thou forgavest the iniquity of my sin." (Psalm 32:5) Actually, all of Psalm 51, 1 John 1:5-10, Galatians 2:20 and 2 Corinthians 7:1 are good Scriptures to remember.

After we have done all four of these steps: recognized and acknowledged our sins, confessed and repented of them, given them over to God and read His Word, we can be confident that He will cleanse us, align our feelings with our faith choices and perform His will through us.

5) At this point, just like the priests, we have "changed our clothes"; we have *put off* our sin and self (our body has been cleansed and our spirit purified) and we have *put on* the "beauty of [Christ's] Holiness." (1 Chronicles 16:29; Psalm 96:7-9; Psalm 29:2)

Now, we can boldly enter His presence and worship Him in the "beauty of [His] holiness." Hebrews 10:19, 22 confirms this, "Having therefore, brethren, *boldness to enter into the holiest* by the blood of Jesus...Let us draw near with a true heart in full assurance of faith, having our hearts sprinkled from an evil conscience, and our bodies washed with pure water."

This is what John means when he says the true worshipers will "worship the Father in spirit and in truth." (John 4:23-24)

Chapter Three
Questions

1) What must we do to "prepare ourselves" to enter the Lord's presence? (Psalm 24:3-4)

2) What does the word *holiness* really mean? (Leviticus 21:6-8) *Holiness* is determined by what?

3) Hebrews 12:14 tells us that until we have a pure heart, no man will ever "see" God. Explain this verse in your own words.

4) Does knowing Scripture backwards and forwards, going to church regularly and praying daily make us holy? Why? Why not? (1 Corinthians 8:1)

5) The *fear of the Lord* means essentially two things. What are they?

6) The cleansing steps mentioned in this chapter will not work unless we have the Spirit of God in us and are "born again." Why?

7) The Word tells us that we are to *put off* our sin and *put on* Christ. What are the practical steps to doing this? (1 John 1:9; Matthew 6:14-15; Romans 12:1; Psalm 103;12; Ephesians 5:26; 1 Chronicles 16:29)

Personal Worship - Entering His Presence

Even as the priests of Solomon's Temple, having washed their hands and feet in the Lavers, sacrificed their offerings on the Brazen Altar and immersed totally in the Molton Sea, could then boldly enter into worship in the Holy Place, we too, having confessed and repented and been cleansed by His Word, can have the boldness to enter the Holy Place of our hearts and present our love as a sweet smelling incense offering to the Lord.

Worship *begins* when we present our bodies to the Lord as a living sacrifice, but it's not consummated until we worship Him in spirit and truth at the altar of our hearts. Presenting our bodies as a living sacrifice is an act of obedience, whereas worshiping Him in the spirit is an act of adoration. Total surrender on the first altar (Brazen Altar) is what makes entrance to the Golden Altar of Incense possible. If you recall, all of Israel had access to the first altar but only the priests had access to the second.

We have been talking about the necessity of being a *sacrifice*, in fact "a living sacrifice." In the Hebrew, the word *sacrifice* has an unusual meaning. It means "to become closely involved in a relationship." In other words, *sacrifice means a gift or a giving up of something for another.* This, of course, is exactly what Jesus Christ did for us—He gave up His Life so that we could live. He was both the supreme sacrifice and the ultimate gift. His death on that cross 2000 years ago is what reconciles us to God today. Consequently, there is nothing more that we need to do in order to be saved, except to receive His gift of Life.

Because of Christ's sacrifice for us, Scripture tells us that the veil between the Holy Place and the Holy of Holies has now been rent (Mark 15:38), so we can boldly enter and present ourselves before the Lord. In other words, because of Jesus' death, we can have direct *access* to the throne room of heaven; nothing prevents or hinders us from communing or fellowshiping with Him.

"And *having* an high priest over the house of God; Let us draw near with a true heart in full assurance of faith, having our hearts sprinkled from an evil conscience, and our bodies washed with pure water." (Hebrews 10:21-22)

Where Are the Changed Hearts?

Therefore, as we have seen, true worship is contingent upon our offering ourselves as a living sacrifice and God then cleansing our flesh and spirit. *In other words, our heart condition matters more in worship than our voice, our good intentions or our actions.* Without a cleansed heart, we simply cannot worship.

It's interesting to note that today worship music sales have skyrocketed, but statistics show us that there are more problems in the Christian body now than ever before. Why? If people are buying worship music, why aren't our lives reflecting this?

The answer is simple. We are praising God, but not truly worshiping Him. We are singing unto Him, making melody in our hearts, but not allowing Him to cleanse our hearts. Again, it all goes back to, most Christians do not know what it means to love God. They don't know how to daily surrender and relinquish themselves to Him. Without this knowledge, not only will there be no changed lives, there also will be no worshipers. And, this is what we are seeing.

If there is no exchange of life (no "beauty of His holiness"), then no matter what we do, we'll have no intimacy with the Lord either. The Holy Spirit is not interested in simply giving us a revelation of Christ, He wants to make us a reproduction of Christ. (Romans 8:29)

Worship, therefore, is not something that is practiced externally but something that is accomplished internally. Richard Foster writes, "Today the heart of God is an open wound of Love. He aches over our distance and preoccupation. He mourns that we do not draw near to Him. He grieves that we have forgotten Him. He weeps over our obsession with muchness and manyness. He longs for our presence."[9]

The above reminds me of the article by Francis Frangipane quoted in the *Introduction* of this book. As a pastor, Francis had become too busy to really worship. As you recall, God communicates to Francis' friend and says, "Tell Francis I miss him." And, it's so true. God grieves over our distance from Him and over our preoccupation with other "more important" things.

Sunday Worship Only

The next question we must address is: When is it appropriate to worship? Do we worship the Lord *only* on Sundays and *only* in public or are we to worship Him daily and privately? And, if so, how do we do it?

How unfortunate to say that we only "worship God" Sunday mornings at 9:30 A.M. If we truly love God, *what happens the other six days of the week?* How can we expect instant worship of God on Sunday mornings when most of us have just spent the last hour and a half yelling at our kids to get ready on time and arguing with our husbands about what we are going to do after

---

[9] *Experiencing God in Worship,* page 73.

church. Then, once we arrive at church, we're not given enough time to go before the Lord and get cleaned up—to get from the Brazen Altar of *sacrifice* to the Incense Altar of *worship*! (Matthew 23:25-26)

Let me read you a letter I received about this very thing. It expresses some very interesting viewpoints. Before reading it, keep in mind the definition of worship which was "to prostrate ourselves, to bow down and *to kiss the Lord*." Here's the letter:

"If we think that Sunday morning is the time we worship, we couldn't be further from the truth. Now, I am not saying that we don't worship in our hearts at that particular point in time. But merely that Sunday mornings are not truly representative of what it means to worship. Do we meet together because it's Sunday and it's the one day of the week where God is asking for a kiss so we must give it? Worse yet, do we give it half-heartedly because we feel "I have to be at church today because I haven't been for weeks." *Sunday morning should be the physical expression of what is happening in our hearts the entire rest of the week.* It's a time when we can all get together corporately and reflect the true state of our hearts.

"I'll use my daughter as an example of the kind of worship that, I believe, God desires. *Nothing gives me more pleasusre than to receive a kiss from her without asking for one.* I love it when she takes me by the hand and wants me to be involved in whatever she is doing. This is how we should view our relationship with our Father in heaven. We should adore Him. We should always be mindful of Him. We should constantly want to interact with Him. Ask Him things. Tell Him our thoughts. Cry our heart out to Him. Set Him above everything else in our lives…"

Worship, then, is simply the act of expressing to the Lord the gift of our Love. It's our time to not only initiate, but also to maintain, an open communion with Him. So, *when* and *how* are we to do this?

Well, we've seen that the priests worshiped the Lord twice a day, everyday. God calls us a priesthood of believers, so shouldn't we try to do the same? "Ye are…a royal priesthood…that should show forth the praises of Him who hath called you out of darkness into His marvelous light." "…Ye also, …a holy priesthood, [should] offer up spiritual sacrifices, acceptable to God by Jesus Christ." And finally, "Jesus Christ hath made us kings and *priests* unto God…" (See Chapter Two.)

Thus, the Lord has given us a model or an example of not only *how* we are to worship, but also *when* we are to worship. Please bear in mind, since we are **not** under the Law, we can, in fact, worship the Lord as little or as much as we like. It doesn't change our salvation. What is affected by our daily encounters with the living God, however, is our personal intimacy with Him, our joy and our strength.

Personal Application

Let's put all of this into practical application.

Let me share with you some of the specific things the Lord has led me to do in my own times of seeking Him. Now, you have the same "Instruction Manual" as I do, so be sure to check out everything I share. If it bears witness, then praise God. If it doesn't, then take what you will from these suggestions and formulate your own special time with Him. The most important thing is to let the Holy Spirit lead you and not let another day go by without beginning to truly worship the Lord.

Twice a day, before 7 a.m. in the morning and after 10 p.m. in the evening (after the phone has stopped ringing and after everyone is in bed), I set aside some special time to seek the Lord. This time has now become the most precious part of my entire day. I find that I can hardly wait for my next encounter with the King. Psalm 73:25 says it perfectly: "There is none upon the earth that I desire beside Thee."

Of course, we can worship the Lord all day long if we want to, but I know in my own life with all the hustle and bustle of my busy schedule, the worship time that I set aside to be totally *alone with Him* in the morning and the evening, is the most blessed of all. Because I'm quiet and I'm listening, He has my full attention. Thus, when He speaks, I'm ready to hear. At the beginning of this special time, I pray and ask the Lord not to allow any thoughts to come into my mind that "are not of Him."

Entering His Courts with Praise

The first place I begin is with praise and thanksgiving, just like the priests in the Outer Court. I was excited to read that David Wilkerson, one of my all-time favorite pastors, also begins his times with the Lord by entering, as he puts it, "God's courts with praise and thanksgiving."[10]

Psalm 100:4 validates this: "*Enter into His gates with thanksgiving, and into His courts with praise: be thankful unto Him,* and bless His Name."

And, Psalm 95:1-2, "O come, let us sing unto the LORD: let us make a joyful noise to the rock of our salvation. Let us come before His presence with thanksgiving, and make a joyful noise unto him with psalms. See also Psalm 118:19 and Isaiah 26:2.

Some other wonderful Psalms for praising God are: Psalms 8, 9, 19, 32, 33, 34, 47, 48, 66, 89, 93, 96, 98, 100,

---

[10] Dave Wilkerson's *Pulpit Series,* "Feeding on Christ" 2/13/02.

101, 104, 105, 111, 112, 113, 115, 118, 134, 135, 136, 138, 144, 145, 146, 147, 148, 149, 150.

The praise Psalms that the priests of Solomon's Temple actually prayed (as they entered the Court) were:[11]

On Sunday - Psalm 24
On Monday - Psalm 48
On Tuesday - Psalm 82
On Wednesday - Psalm 94
On Thursday - Psalm 81
On Friday - Psalm 93
On Saturday - Psalm 92

Look these up. They're great!

Praising God for Who He Is

It's helpful to know some of the specific names and characteristics of Jesus, so you can praise Him for who He is and for what He has done in your life. Meditate upon each of these names as you pray them. Again, always let the Holy Spirit guide you.

Alpha and Omega
Almighty
Anchor of My Soul
Advocate

---

[11] *A House of Prayer for all Nations,* Chaim Richman, page 48.

Avenger of Blood
Anointed One
All and In All
Author and Finisher of My Faith
Bread of Life
Beloved
Blessed Above All
Bright and Morning Star
Bishop of My Soul
Creator
Counselor
Crown
Companion
Cornerstone of My Faith
Comforter
Consolation
Dwelling Place
Delight
Deliverer
Defender
Desire
Emmanuel (God with us)
Everlasting Father
Eternal One
Friend
Faithful One
Father
Fountain of Life
Firstborn

Foundation
Glory
Guide
Guilt-taker
Hiding Place
Holy One
Hoshana
Husband
Healer
Hope
Helper
Horn of My Salvation
I Am
Image of God
Immanuel
Joy
King
Lamb of God
Lord of Lords
Light
Lion
Love
Life
Master
Messiah
Most High
Mouth
Mercy
Name Above All Names

Overcomer
Prophet
Priest
Prince of Peace
Great Physician
Preserver
Passover
Peace
Power
Prize
Pearl
Precious One
Perfect One
Pure One
Redeemer
Righteous
Refuge
Ruler
Resurrection
Ransom
Root of David
Redemption
River of Life
Rock
Rewarder
Restorer
Savior
Spirit
Sanctification
Strength

Sufficiency
Standard
Salvation
Son of David
Son of God
Son of Man
Living Stone
Suffering Servant
Shepherd of My Soul
Sacrifice
Shekinah Glory
Shiloh
Sceptre
Song
Triumph
Teacher
Treasure
Tabernacle
Truth
Unspeakable Gift
Unchangeable
Unleavened Bread
Vindication
Victory
Voice
Worth
Way
Wonderful
Wisdom

Things To Be Thankful For

After I have praised Him, I begin to thank Him for all the things I can think of that He has done for me. The following are a few suggestions. Again, let the Holy Spirit add to your list:

Jesus, I am thankful:

For Your soon coming—my hope
For my salvation—for Your Life in me
For being Your beloved (whether I feel like it or not)
For my relationship with You—the freedom You have given me
For Your Strength, Your Love, Your Wisdom, Your Power
For Your presence—our intimacy, fellowship and communion
For Your discernment and guidance
For Your rest, Your joy and Your peace
For continually cleansing me by Your blood— Your restoration
For Your protection
For my spouse
For my children
For my family
For my friends
For my health

For my home
For my situation—no matter what difficulties I face
For what You are doing through me
For the people I work with
For my job

After the priests finished praising and thanking God, they entered the Inner Court and went through the ritual of cleansing that we spoke about in the last chapter. In like manner, *before* I can enter the Holy Place, I, too, must recognize my sin and self; confess and repent of it (and also choose to forgive anyone who has wronged me); surrender the things the Lord has shown me; and then replace them with His Word. (Again, see *The Key* or re-read Chapter Three.)

Personal Worship in The Holy Place

Once I have *put off* my sin and self, then I can proceed into the Holy Place where I can "change my clothes," just like the priests. This is where I *put on* Christ–exchange lives with Him–and where I *put on* the beauty of His holiness and receive the boldness to enter His presence.

Hebrews 10:19 and 22 tell us, "Having therefore, brethren, boldness to enter into the holiest by the blood of Jesus...Let us draw near with a true heart in full assurance of faith, having our hearts sprinkled from an evil conscience, and our bodies washed with pure water."

At this point, I picture myself carrying from the Brazen Altar those hot coals of my wholly burnt life right into the Holy Place and the Incense Altar where God has promised to "meet with me." (Exodus 25:22) Because I now have "clean hands (a pure heart)," I can worship Him not only in "*the beauty of holiness,*" but also in spirit and truth. "The hour is coming and now is, when the true worshipers shall worship the Father in spirit and in truth, for the Father seeks such to worship Him. God is a Spirit and they that worship Him must worship Him in spirit and truth." (John 4:23-24)

It was at this point that the priests sprinkled incense over the hot coals, fell on their faces and worshiped the Lord. In Revelation 4:8 and 11, they do the same. "Holy, Holy, Holy, Lord God Almighty, which was and is and is to come…Thou art worthy, O Lord to receive glory and honour and power; for Thou has created all things and for Thy pleasure they are and were created."

And it's the same with us. Again, Psalm 95:6-7, "Oh, come, let us worship and bow down; let us kneel before the Lord our maker. For He is our God, and we are the people of His pasture, and the sheep of His hand…"

Consumed in His Presence

At this point I take off my shoes, sprinkle incense over a candle that I have just lit, and prostrate myself on the floor before the Lord. Now, there's nothing special about lighting a candle or sprinkling incense, except that to me it represents my "being one" with my Lord. The incense represents my love for Him, and the fire from the candle represents His Love for me. So, at that moment, the fire and incense represents our becoming one.

I play my favorite worship music and begin to worship Him in the Spirit. There seems to be an intrinsic bond between music and worship. Psalm 100:2 tells us, "[we are to] come before His presence with singing." Music and worship just go together. Music is the doorway to our hearts. (Ephesians 5:19) At this point, I either sing along with the music, pray in the Spirit or just lie before Him in silent adoration. I'm not asking Him for anything nor seeking to hear Him; I'm just there to adore, revere and worship Him.

Being in His presence often reduces me to sobbing, not for any sadness on my part, but simply because I am overwhelmed with joy. The Creator of the universe is before me and He cares about me. It's staggering when you really think about what is happening! As Psalm 16:11 tells us, "...only in His presence is fullness of joy."

I feel surrounded by the thought of heaven and the Lord sitting before me reaching out. Worship is like the *bridge* between this world and the next. When we worship, we can almost touch the coming kingdom. Having lost our son Chip, who loved the Lord, just three years ago and last year my Mom, who came to know the Lord deeply after Chip's death, one night while I was worshiping, I could almost see them there with Jesus. It sounds mysterious, but worship is what propels us into His presence with a glimpse of heaven.

For those few moments the joy of being before Him becomes overwhelming and nothing else matters in the entire world. I am "joined" with my Lord in the Spirit and lost in the joy of His presence. At this point, my spirit is raised to heights that it has never before known. Just as the incense and the cloud of Divine Glory were intermingled above the Golden Altar in Solomon's Temple, for those few moments I, too, am *intertwined with my Lord in the Spirit.* Because of this incredible experience, I can now understand the definition of "worship" a little more clearly: *"being on fire and completely consumed in His Love."*

I am reminded of 2 Chronicles 5:13-14 which says, "It came even to pass, as the trumpeters and singers were as one, to make one sound to be heard in praising and thanking the Lord; and when they lifted up their voice with the trumpets and cymbals and instruments of music and praised the Lord, saying, For He is good; for His mercy endureth forever, that then the house was filled with a cloud, even the house of the Lord. So that the priests could not stand to minister by reason of the cloud; *for the glory of the Lord had filled the house of God.*

In a small way I feel exactly as those priests did.

Now, my encounters with the Lord are <u>not</u> always dramatic. Sometimes, I worship Him and don't feel nor see a thing, but I still *know* He is there and that He hears and is pleased. Other times, my time with Him is electric!

Using Scriptures in Worship

I will often repeat 1 Chronicles 29:10-13 over and over again from my heart:

"Blessed be Thou, Lord God of Israel, our father, forever and ever. Thine, O Lord, is the greatness, and the power, and the glory and the victory, and the majesty; for all that is in the heaven and in the earth is Thine. Thine is the kingdom, O Lord, and Thou art exalted as head above all. Both riches and honor come of Thee, and Thou reignest over all, and in thine hand is power and might; and in Thine hand it is to make great, and to give strength unto all. Now, therefore, our God, we thank Thee and praise Thy glorious Name."

Or, I will repeat certain phrases from Revelation:

"Holy, holy, holy, Lord God Almighty, which was, and is, and is to come." (Revelation 4:8b)

"Thou art worthy, O Lord, to receive glory and honour and power: for thou hast created all things, and for thy pleasure they are and were created." (Revelation 4:11)

"Worthy is the Lamb that was slain to receive power, and riches, and wisdom, and strength, and honour, and glory, and blessing....Blessing, and honour, and glory, and power, *be* unto Him that sitteth upon the throne, and unto the Lamb for ever and ever." (Revelation 5:12-13)

"Blessing, and glory, and wisdom, and thanksgiving, and honour, and power, and might, *be* unto our God for ever and ever." (Revelation 7:12)

"The kingdoms of this world are become *the kingdoms* of our Lord, and of His Christ; and He shall reign for ever and ever...We give thee thanks, O Lord God Almighty, which art, and wast, and art to come; because Thou hast taken to Thee Thy great power, and hast reigned." (Revelation 11:15 and 17)

"Great and marvellous *are* thy works, Lord God Almighty; just and true *are* thy ways, thou King of saints.

...For Thou only *art* holy..." (Revelation 15:3-4).

"Thou art righteous, O Lord, which art, and wast, and shalt be..." (Revelation 16:5)

Or, I read one of my favorite worship passages. See Psalm 72:17-19; 91; 95:1-7; 96:1-9; 113; 134; 135; 136; 145; 150.

I continue to let the Spirit lead me and do whatever He tells me. Sometimes I raise my hands, sometimes I'm on my knees, and, sometimes, I'm flat on my face, silently kissing and holding the Lord in the Spirit. Again at that moment, "...there is none upon the earth that I desire beside Thee." (Psalm 73:25)

Divine Revelation

Worship releases blessings in two directions. Not only are we loving God, but He is extending His Love back towards us. Thus, part of the joy of worship is the divine revelation that often results.

Intimacy, however, must always precede insight.

In Dave Hunt's latest newsletter, he comments: "Appreciation begets worship, and the Lord responds by revealing Himself in ever greater measure in a fellowship of love that overflows in fruitful witnessing."[12]

---

[12] *The Berean Call,* "One Thing," May 2002.

God gave us worship so that we might become partakers of His highest purposes. Yes, Christ is the major focus of our worship, but as we worship He often reveals His plans and His purposes for our lives. Worship, therefore, is not only the means to His presence but also to His revelation. In worship, He desires to:

1)   make His presence known,
2)   reveal His person to us,
3)   reveal His power to us,
4)   reveal His eternal purposes to us,
5)   reveal His personal plans for our lives.

When I am worshiping, I find it necessary to have my Bible and my journal close at hand. Of course, God works differently in each of our lives. But, for me, He seems to make His presence known *through His Word*. Thus, if I don't have my journal handy to write down what I hear, by the time I'm through worshiping, I will have forgotten it.

I was interested to read what Bob Sorge, again in his book *Secrets of the Secret Place*, says about writing things down. "I am personally convinced that I cannot hold onto what God gives me apart from writing it down…Those who retain what God gives them will be given more."

I agree with this wholeheartedly.

Our Response to the Revelation of His Love

The response that the Lord desires from us after we have been in His presence is to:

1) See ourselves as we truly are, experience contrition, brokenness, sorrow, shame, grief, repentance and honesty and to have an open and a contrite heart.
2) Submit and dedicate ourselves to Him to an even greater degree—yielding, surrendering and sacrificing ourselves to His will, His Word and His authority. (Isaiah 6:8; James 1:21-25).
3) Have an urgency to lay our burdens, requests and intercessory prayers at His feet and be propelled to pray even more for the lost, the divisions, the injustices, the diseased, the pain and the difficulties others are experiencing. (Philippians 4:6; Ephesians 6:18; 1 Timothy 2: 1-3; Mark 14, Matthew 26, Luke 22, John 13 and 1 Corinthians 11)
4) And lastly, to love, adore, enjoy, honor, exalt, magnify, glorify and praise Christ even more than we are doing now.

"Holy, holy, holy, *is* the LORD of hosts: the whole earth *is* full of His glory." (Isaiah 6:3)

Overcome by "the Joy of our Salvation"

The bottom line is that: *experiencing the manifestation of His presence—through His Word, through His Spirit or through just knowing He is present—fills us with indescribable joy, no matter what our circumstances are!*

This kind of encounter is what restores the joy of our salvation. This joy only comes as a result of adoring, loving and worshiping the Lord in spirit and in truth. Experiencing His presence, regardless of our situation, is what "brightens us up," gives us hope and allows us to go on. We've finally become one in spirit with Him.

This rejoicing at the manifestation of the Lord, is what gives us our strength. As Nehemiah 8:10 reminds us, *joy is what leads us to strength.* And that strength comes only as a result of becoming one with Him—for it's *His* strength. In other words, overwhelming joy and supernatural strength arise out of a deeper personal revelation of who God is.

Is this only to be done on Sundays and in church? I think not!

Worshiping the Lord like this is what brings about a "spirit of meekness" and humility—a true sign of Christ-likeness. If we can be meek in our spirit before the Lord, He, then, will enable us to be humble before others in our lives. As Isaiah 29:19 says, "The meek shall increase their joy in the Lord..."

Chapter Four
Questions

1) What does the term *sacrifice* really mean? In light of this definition, what does it mean to be a "living" sacrifice? (Romans 12:1)   Of what does this avail us?

2) Why do we see so few true changed hearts these days? What is the real problem?

3) Is worship something that we do *externally* or *internally*? Explain your answer. Why?

4) Why is it not enough to worship the Father only on Sundays at 11a.m. What is your own habit of wor-

ship? Do you plan any future changes? Why? Why not?

5) What does the Psalm 73:25 personally mean to you? "There is none upon the earth that I desire beside Thee."

6) What is it that will give us the "boldness to enter the holiest place"? (Hebrews 10:19)

7) What are some of your own favorite worship Scriptures? 1 Chronicles 29:10-13 is one of mine.

8) Worship releases blessings in two directions. What are they? What revelation of love has the Lord ministered to you lately?

9) How does God want us to respond to His revelation of love? (Isaiah 6:3, 8; Philippians 4:6)

10) What is it that restores the joy of our salvation? (Psalm 51:11-12) Consequently, what is it that gives us our strength? (Nehemiah 8:10)

5

Incense and Intimacy - Hearing His Voice

Oneness with the Lord

Our soul's natural strength is dealt with on the Brazen Altar, but it's not until we reach the Incense Altar that God is truly able to rule and reign in our lives. *The Incense Altar symbolizes the complete union of our spirit with His Spirit.* It represents our oneness, our communion and our intercourse with Him. Our spirit has been strengthened so that it can now freely direct our soul in all things. This is the way God intended us to live from the very beginning.

Two containers or two wills in one body will never work! God wants us to be "one," not only *positionally*, but also *experientially*, even if it's only for a few moments. Perhaps tomorrow we'll be able to do it for an even longer period of time, and the day after, even longer still. Only Jesus was able to stay in this perfect communion.

Union with Christ—a deeper merging of our spirits—becomes the climax of our relationship with Him. This is the completion, the perfection and the fulness of God that He has designed for every one of us. Everything on the *inside* and everything on the *outside* has finally become His.

Now, please don't misunderstand me. It's not as if we become God or even "little gods" because of our union with Him. Just as the perfume retained its own unique properties, but was simply united, mingled, fused and joined with the cloud of fire, so we retain our individuality and our humanness when we are united with God.

An analogy that might help give us more understanding of this paradox is: the Incense Altar sat physically in the Holy Place just *outside* the veil to the Holy of Holies. However, it was always considered to be a part of the Holy of Holies. Listen to Leviticus 16:12-13, "And he shall take a censer full of burning coals of fire from off the altar before the Lord [Brazen Altar], and his hands full of sweet incense beaten small, and *bring it within the veil*: And he shall put the incense upon *the fire before the Lord*, that the cloud of the incense may cover the mercy seat that is upon the testimony..."

Also, Hebrews 9:3-5, "And *after the second veil*, the tabernacle which is called the Holiest of all; Which had *the golden censer*, and the ark of the covenant overlaid round about with gold, wherein *was* the golden pot that had manna, and Aaron's rod that budded, and the tables of the covenant; And over it the cherubims of glory shadowing the mercy seat..." (Hebrews 9:3-5)

In like manner, we are considered *positionally* to be one with the Lord. However, *experientially* it's a whole other story.

As John 17 expresses it, "...That they all may be one; as Thou, Father, art in Me, and I in Thee, that they also may be *one in us*...Father, I will that they also, whom Thou hast given Me, *be with Me where I am*, that they may behold My glory, which Thou hast given Me...." (verses 21, 24)

Offering of the Incense

Incense means "to blow or to breathe." Throughout Scripture, it was called "sweet smoke." Incense represents our praise, our prayers and our worship. In the Bible incense was always associated with the temple and with worship. Revelation 8:3-4 explains, "And another angel came and stood at the altar, having a golden censer; and there was given unto him much incense, that he should offer *it* with the prayers of all saints upon *the golden altar which was before the throne*. And the smoke of the incense, which came with the prayers of the saints, ascended up before God..." (See also Psalm 141:2.)

Malachi 1:11, however, tells us that in the end times "...[His] Name shall be great among the Gentiles, and *in every place incense shall be offered unto [His] Name.*" In other words, in these end times God wants all Christians everywhere and in every place to offer incense to His Name. It doesn't matter *who* we are or *where* we are, the Lord wants us to seek Him, to offer incense and to worship Him.

Thus, carrying that hot piece of coal as a symbol of our crucified life, placing it on the Incense Altar, and watching as the perfume and the fire become one, is a graphic picture of what it means to worship Him. As we offer God the incense of our wholly burnt lives, we become "one" just like fire and wood.[13]

Another analogy is the pillar of cloud and fire in the Old Testament. (Exodus 13:21) The intertwined cloud and fire always stood as a symbol of God's presence. That same pillar of cloud and fire, the Shekinah Glory, dwelt in the Holy of Holies in Solomon's Temple. And, when the incense was offered, the perfume cloud intermingled with the Shekinah Glory and became a pleasing aroma unto the Lord.

Incense represents the *fragrance of a life.* A bad savor means an unholy or impure life; a good savor means a holy or pure life. When sin and self no longer form a barrier preventing our approach to God, then a sweet

---

[13] See *The Way of Agape,* Chapter Eight.

aroma can come up before Him. In other words, when we become "one" with Him we radiate the fragrance of His Life.

That incense—that sweet fragrance of holiness—rises up to God as an acceptable offering. It's the product of our sanctification and our purification. 2 Corinthians 2:15 tells us that "we are unto God a sweet savor of Christ." That sweet fragrance "before the Lord" assures us access to His throne.

Our prayers are also said to ascend unto God as sweet incense. (Psalm 141:2; Acts 10:4) Revelation 8:3 explains, "And another angel came and stood at the altar, having a golden censer; and there was given unto him much incense, that he should offer it with the prayers of all saints upon the *Golden Altar which was before the throne.*"

The Place God Meets With Us

The Old Testament precept, "Thou shall put it [the incense] *before* the veil that is by the ark of the testimony...*where I will meet with You*" was fulfilled when the priests put incense on the Golden Altar before the veil. (Exodus 25:22) Again, that incense was the result of a sacrifice already given. Interestingly, it was *never* presented to the Lord without *first* being completely burnt. It was beaten small and then presented before

Him on the altar where He promised to meet with them. (Leviticus 16:12) Likewise, we are able to "meet with Him" when we allow God to humble us ("be made small"). Then, we are able to bring the love that remains before Him in utter and complete adoration.

One of the reasons God created the sanctification process in the first place, was so that He might bring us near to Him. Numbers 16:9 validates this: "Seemeth it but a small thing unto you, that the God of Israel *hath separated you* [consecrated you] from the congregation of Israel, *to bring you near to Himself*...."

Scripture also tells us that there are three different places in the temple that God met with the priests: 1) at the Ark of the Covenant in the Holy of Holies (Exodus 25:22); 2) at the Incense Altar in the Holy Place (Exodus 30:6, 36); and, 3) at the Brazen Altar in the Inner Court (Exodus 29:42). Note that each room of the temple is represented here. In like manner, even when we "feel" alone and abandoned in difficult times, *God promises to be there with us in the midst of the fire. And, He promises never to leave or forsake us.*

Two-Way Communication

We said earlier that worship is a two-way communication. When we humble ourselves, love and worship God, He then hears, answers and reveals Himself to us. Here's a personal example:

Recently I was experiencing an extremely difficult situation. I was embroiled in some circumstances that didn't seem to have a solution. During one of my worship times, God gave me an incredible Scripture. It was one I had never seen before, and it fit my situation perfectly! "Though you have lien among the pots [in back rooms], yet shall you be as the wings of a dove covered with silver...." (Psalm 68:13)

This little verse expressed God's personal voice to me and made me realize that He cared, even about this insignificant circumstance in my life. That knowledge carried me through some further stressful times. It also gave me the hope that He knew exactly what was occurring in my life and that He would bring me through.

Which, of course, He did magnificently in the end.

A Scriptural example of this very same thing is Moses in Numbers 20:6-7. God not only spoke face to face with Moses, He allowed him to see His glory. As a result, Moses was changed. He received just enough hope to carry him through the difficult times ahead.

And the same is true for us. God reveals Himself not only to give us the strength to continue on but also the encouragement to worship more. When Moses saw the revelation of God's glory, Scripture tells us he immediately fell to his knees and worshiped. Then he went on to pray, "O Lord, let my Lord, I pray Thee, go among us; ...and pardon our iniquity and our sin..." (Exodus 34:8-9) In other words, that revelation of God's glory not only changed Moses, but it also gave him God's heart. It prompted him to have personal concern and compassion for others.

This is the first incident that mentions Moses "worshiping the Lord." Before this, Scripture tells us that Moses prayed, interceded, wept and pleaded with God, but it never speaks of him worshiping. In other words, something unique happened here. Moses saw God's glory and it caused him to worship! One is the source of the other. *Seeing the manifestation of God's glory births more worship in us.* Deeper intimacy arises out of a growing revelation of who God is. (Exodus 24:9-18; 33:11-22)

Consequently, the manifestation of God's glory not only leads to deeper heartfelt worship, but also to more intercession for others.

Praying our Petitions

John 9:31 tells us that "God hears true worshipers." Thus, those who become one with the Lord by worshiping, can be assured that He will hear and answer their prayers.

Just as the perfume of incense and the cloud of Glory intermingled and became one above the Golden Altar in the Temple of Solomon, when we worship the Lord we become united in love and one in spirit. John 16:24 tells us that at this moment we can ask whatever we will and the Lord promises to hear us. We haven't just verbally attached "in His Name" to our prayers, *we are literallly joined and united "in His Name" while we are praying.* Big difference! And because we are "one," He promises to hear and answer. Thus, our prayers will not only be according to His will but, also, our "joy will be full."

A Praying and Worshiping Man

King David is a perfect example of a worshiping and praying man. Scripture tells us that nothing could take him away from his times of prayer with the Lord. Prayer and worship was David's central occupation. Three times a day, He came before the Lord to spend time with Him.

Because of this intimacy, David didn't have to turn to others to tell him what he should do. He was so united with the Lord ("in His Name"), that the Lord freely answered his prayers and personally told him what to do.

Daniel is another example of one who was at one with the Lord. Daniel was so beloved by God that the angel Gabriel came and told him that the Lord had given him special skill and understanding. (Daniel 9:21-23) What a glorious message from God Himself! Wouldn't you just love to receive a word like that from the Creator of the universe? Wouldn't that give you exceeding joy, beyond anything you could ever think or imagine?

Nebuchadnezzar, on the other hand, was not a praying or worshiping man, and, thus, he had to continually seek other people to tell him what to do. He had all the power and all the influence of an empire, and yet he had no peace, no answers and no joy from the Lord.

Praying the Scriptures

I learned long ago that if I wanted anything at all to be accomplished, it must be brought before the Lord in prayer. I also learned, however, that there is an appropriate *way* to pray and an appropriate *time* to pray laid out for us in Scripture. When I followed the Lord's prescribed instructions, tremendous results occurred. When I didn't, everything would fall apart! Again, God makes the rules; our duty is simply to follow them.

Someone taught me years ago that when *I prayed the Scriptures,* God would do powerful things, not only in me, but also in the ones I was praying for. Bob Sorge, again in his book *Secrets of the Secret Place,* states "when we pray with God's Word on our lips, we know we are praying prayers that are living and powerful."

Hebrews 4:12 validates this. "For the word of God *is* quick, and powerful, and sharper than any two-edged sword, piercing even to the dividing asunder of soul and spirit, and of the joints and marrow, and *is* a discerner of the thoughts and intents of the heart."

And, it's true! "When the language of our prayers is shaped by the Scriptures, we gain confidence in knowing that we are praying according to the will of God." This way we by-pass our own self-centered, pity-party prayers and step into God's thoughts, His mind and His wisdom. Now, there's no reason to be afraid of repetition. God knows our heart and what is important to us and by repeating our prayers we become like that persistent friend in Luke 11 who would not take "no" for an answer.

Again, be sure to have your Bible handy when you go into worship and prayer. Then, you not only can pray the Scriptures, but the Lord can also speak His will back to you through the Scriptures.

Since it's always been very difficult for me to memorize Scripture, I found writing the Scriptures out and then praying them, to be extremely helpful and beneficial. So, the following Scriptures are simply suggestions for prayer. They are not intended to be an in-depth thesis on prayer and worship. They are simply some personal thoughts and ideas that have helped me in my over-45-year walk with the Lord. Again, if they minister, wonderful! If not, skip them and continue reading. Just as in worship, it's imperative to allow the Holy Spirit to direct your prayers.

Remember, we are not under the law, but under grace. Therefore, I do not mean to imply a "methodology" or a "ritual" here. We don't have to "work our way to heaven." However, I do believe God has given us His Word and He is very pleased when we pray it back to Him.

Personal Prayers

Some personal prayers that have ministered to me over the years are:

Psalm 139:23-24 - Search me and know my heart and my thoughts. See if there be any wicked way in me and lead me in Your way.

Job 34:32 - That which I cannot see, please teach me.

Psalm 45:17 - I desire to make Your Name be remembered in all generations.

Psalm 17:2 - Let my sentence come forth only from Your presence.

Ephesians 4:29-31 - Let no corrupt communication proceed out of my mouth, but that which is good to the use of edifying, that it may minister grace to the hearer. Let me not grieve the Holy Spirit, whereby I am sealed. Let all bitterness and wrath and anger and clamor and evil speaking be put away from me with all malice, etc....

Ephesians 4:32 - Be kind to one another, tender hearted, forgiving one another, just as Christ has forgiven me.

Hebrews 4:16 - Let me come boldly to Your throne in time of need and find mercy.

Psalm 119:133 - Order my steps in Your Word. Don't let sin or self have dominion over me.

Romans 4:21 - I choose to be *fully persuaded* that what You have promised me, You will perform.

1 Corinthians 2:2 - I pray that I would know nothing but "Christ crucified."

Philippians 4:19 - That You would supply all my needs according to Your riches in glory.

Matthew 22:37 - I desire to love You with all my heart, with all my will and with all my soul, so that I can then love my neighbor as myself.

Romans 12:1-2 - I offer my body as a living sacrifice, holy and acceptable which is my reasonable service, and I choose <u>not</u> to be conformed to this world, but to be transformed into Your Image (and show forth Your Life) by *the renewing of my mind*, so that I can, then, prove in my actions what is the good, the acceptable and the perfect will of God.

Psalm 138:3 - Make me bold with Your strength in my soul.

Galatians 1:16 - May You reveal Yourself in me, so that I might speak as You would have me.

Joshua 9:25 - I am in Your hands, do what You will with me. Have Your way in me.

Philemon 14 - Without Your opinion, I will do nothing.

Acts 2:28 - That You would make me full of joy with Your countenance.

Colossians 3:4 - Christ, You are my life.

Philippians 1:21 - For me to live is Christ.

Family Prayers

In addition to your own daily prayers for each member of your family, here are some further Scriptures you might want to pray for them. (Again, let the Holy Spirit pick which ones.)

Ephesians 1:17-19 - I pray for Your Spirit of wisdom and revelation for _____. I pray that the eyes of his understanding would be enlightened, so that he might know the hope of Your calling, the riches of Your inheritance, and the exceeding greatness of Your Power towards them who believe.

Ephesians 3:16-19 - I pray_____will be strengthened with might by Your Spirit in the inner man; that You might dwell in his heart and that he might be rooted and grounded in Your Love and able to comprehend the breadth, the depth and the height of Your Love, so that he might be filled up with the fulness of You.

Philippians 3:10 - I pray that_____may know You and the power of Your resurrection and the fellowship of Your sufferings, so that he might be made conformable to Your Image.

2 Timothy 2:25 - I pray that You would give_____ repentance to the acknowledging of the truth.

Think also about praying: Acts 16:31; 1 Kings 8:23-53; Daniel 9:3-19; and, Colossians 1:9.

Other Suggested Prayers for Loved Ones

Someone once gave me this list to pray for others. As I tried it, I was amazed to see so many I prayed for changed.

Pray that God would "lift the veil" and give them a personal revelation of Jesus.

Pray that the Holy Spirit would continue to hover over them and give them supernatural protection.

Pray that God would put godly people in their path.
Pray that God would expose all pride and rebelliousness.

Pray that God would expose all their hidden thought patterns—religious prejudices, known strongholds and evil spirits, etc.

Pray that God would bind Satan from taking them captive.

Pray that He would place His armor around them, and that He would do all He could to bring them to Himself.[14]

---

[14] Taken, in part, from the book *Intercessory Prayer* by Dutch Sheets.

P.S. I might also suggest making a special prayer notebook or prayer journal with all of your own special Scriptures. Then, you can take it into the prayer closet with you. My prayer diary goes everywhere with me. Those who have seen it laugh, because it is so dog-eared and so beat up. Never mind, I know what it says and it helps me remember the Scriptures.

Lingering in His Presence

David Wilkerson, again one of my favorite pastors, says, "After I end my prayer time, I linger in my secret closet of prayer. I bow before the Lord and say, 'Jesus, I'm here just for You. I don't bring any more requests or petitions. This is Your time and Yours alone. I'm here to listen to Your heart.'"

He goes on to say "I simply stay in His presence, loving Him and waiting on Him. I know He will come to me and speak His Mind."[15]

Just like the priests of Solomon's Temple, when their worship and prayer time was over, they went out and ministered to the congregation. We, too, at this point, can go out and share of the fulness of the Lord that we have received while worshiping Him at the altar of our hearts. By doing this, we will bless those we come in contact with by *His* continuing presence in us.

---

[15] "Feeding on Christ," *The Pulpit Series,* 2/13/02

Chapter Five
Questions

1) In our little overview of the temple worship, what does the Incense Altar symbolize? Why is it the climax of our relationship with the Lord? Explain.

2) What does incense stand for? (Isaiah 60:6) In the "end times" *where* shall it be offered? (Malachi 1:11)

3) Where are the three places that God tells us in Scripture "He will meet with us"? (Exodus 25:22; 30:34-37; Leviticus 16:12)

4) How does our two way communication with the Lord work? We humble ourselves and love and extol Him; He then, does what?

5) Give a Scriptural example of one who heard God's voice and was changed by that encounter. How can we be assured that God will hear our own prayers? Why is keeping a special prayer journal so important?

6) Deeper intimacy arises out of what? (Exodus 34:8)

7) Give several Scriptural examples of men or women who enjoyed intimacy with the Lord and *why* they did so. Give examples of men or women who did not and what was the result?

Spiritual Warfare - Vital For Worship

Spiritual Warfare?

If this is a book about entering God's presence and worshiping Him, then why on earth have a chapter about spiritual warfare? We do so because if we are going to be worshipers of God, more than ever before we need to be knowledgeable in spiritual warfare. We need to know about the enemy, his tactics and his ways, because, believe me, we are going to need them![16] If we want to survive these "end times," we really have no other option than to learn *how* to fight the enemy–how to do warfare for ourselves as well as all those for whom we pray.

Therefore, part of our prayer time in the Holy Place *must* be concerned with loosing the strongholds, commanding the enemy to leave and binding ourselves to God's will, His thoughts and His ways.

The Enemy's Involvement

When we are lukewarm Christians and have only a "form of godliness" (2 Timothy 3:5), the devil doesn't seem to bother with us. Why should he, we're no real

---

[16] In the book *The Holy Temple of Jerusalem* by Chaim Rickman, it says that the Incense Altar was "instrumental in subduing evil." (Page 27)

threat to anyone, least of all him. As my Chuck often says, "Many of us are *undercover Christians*—i.e., no one knows we are." So the enemy leaves us alone. But let us begin to worship and love the Lord with all our heart, mind and soul. Then, watch out! We're in for a battle!

Remember how the Israelites tried to stone Joshua and Caleb for their commitment to "go all the way" with God? (Numbers 13:30-14:10) Well, it will be the same with us. Instead of our friends rejoicing or understanding what has happened to us, they'll think we are crazy. They'll ridicule us, mock us and even call us fanatics. You watch, the enemy will find many holes in which to attack us!

Jesus warned us in John 16:2, "These things have I spoken unto you, that ye should not be offended. They shall put you out of the synagogues: yea, the time cometh, that whosoever killeth you will think that he doeth God service. And these things will they do unto you, because they have not known the Father, nor Me."

Why is it that when we decide to surrender everything to the Lord, we automatically become huge targets? When we become worshipers, it's almost as if we develop a great big *bull's eye* on our chest that says, "I love God, shoot me!" The reason this happens is that our mortal enemy not only hates God, but he also hates anyone who wants to follow Him. If we are lukewarm, he won't bother with us. But if we are "hot," watch out, we'll become immediate targets. Satan will do anything he can to thwart God's plans *in* us and *through* us, even to the sending of "angels of light."

Thus, if you intend to learn to worship the Lord, then you must be prepared to fight the enemy, and that involves spiritual warfare.

How Do We Fight?

Okay. How do we fight?

We fight by *surrendering*! Yes, you read that correctly. We learn to fight the enemy by surrendering ourselves more—*not to him*, but to the Lord.

Again, look at Moses. Moses endured such horrendous chiding, testing and humiliation. How did he handle this? What did he do? He withstood the enemy by simply not letting doubt, unbelief, fear, insecurity, bitterness, guilt, etc., consume him, but instead chose to surrender everything to the Lord and trust Him even more. During his difficult trials, Moses shut himself up on that mountain top, prayed, worshiped and looked only to the Lord for His wisdom. (Exodus 5:22-6:7; 19:3-25; 33:12-22) In the end, because of Moses' complete obedience to the Lord's will, the enemy was defeated and he was able to lead a whole nation to freedom. Another example is Stephen who, even as the Israelites were stoning him, looked, prayed and called upon the Lord. Acts 6:15 explains, "all that sat in the council, looking steadfastly on him, *saw his face as it had been the face of an angel.*" See also Acts 7:59.

Again, how did Stephen do this? He did it by having such unshakable faith in the Lord that he was able to "see" Him in the midst of the fire. Just like Moses, he "endured, as seeing Him who is invisible." (Hebrews 11:27)

A further example was the miracle of Job, who in spite of his incredible difficulties, continued to cry out, "Though You slay me, yet will I trust You." (Job 13:15) And finally, there was Paul who, at times, felt lost, confused and bewildered because of all the rejection, mockery, malicious gossip and persecutions that he experienced. He even came to a point of "despairing of life itself." (2 Corinthians 1:8) But the way he handled those things was *not* to give in to defeat but to believe and act out 2 Corinthians 4:8-9:

"We are troubled on every side, yet not distressed; we are perplexed, but not in despair; persecuted, but not forsaken; cast down, but not destroyed; *always bearing about in the body the dying of the Lord Jesus, [so] that the life also of Jesus might be made manifest in our body.*"

All these renowned men not only endured huge trials in their lives, but conquered them. And they did so by surrendering themselves even further to the Lord and recognizing the enemy's involvement. As a result, they were enabled to go on, filled with an inner peace that God's will was being accomplished.

One of the reasons God allows hard times in our lives is to strengthen our faith. (See our book *Faith in the Night Seasons*.) He arranges difficult situations so that we can see *for ourselves* how very weak our faith is. Remember in Deuteronomy 8:2, God reprimanded the Israelites, telling them that He had tested them so that they might see (for themselves) their own hearts and their own unbelief. God is constantly doing the same with us—testing, proving, stretching and enlarging our faith, because our faith is the foundation of our walk. It's what our worship is built upon.

It's also true that if our faith is weak, it's a sure thing we won't be able to stand against the enemy of our souls. If our faith is strong, then there's no end to what God can do through us. Remember Moses, Stephen, Job and Paul, to mention a few.

In truth, if we are not being "stretched," we're not really growing! Real faith is made up of a series of choices (see our new book, *Against the Tide*)—choices to cleanse our hearts of all sin and self; choices to trust

God regardless of our circumstances; and, choices to rely upon His ability to implement His will in our lives. These are the same kind of faith choices that Moses, Stephen, Job and Paul had to face in their own situations. At the time, they certainly didn't "feel like" making these choices, but they knew that their lives depended upon it, so they made them anyway "by faith." And these are the same kinds of faith choices that we must make in order to have peace and joy in the middle of our trials.

Then, we, too, can be *troubled, perplexed, persecuted and cast down, but _not_ distressed, in despair, forsaken or destroyed.*

The Battle is Not Ours, But the Lord's

God tells us in 2 Chronicles 20:15 that "the battle is not ours, but the Lord's." We must continually remember this. Otherwise, we'll end up confused and afraid.

Do you recall the story of Elijah?

1 Kings 18 tells the story of a severe drought. In the third year of the drought, the Lord said to Elijah, "Go and present yourself to King Ahab and tell him I will soon send rain." Elijah did as he was told and asked the king to bring all the people of Israel to Mt. Carmel, along with 450 prophets of Baal and 400 priests of

Ashorah, who were supported by Jezebel, the king's wife. Elijah wanted to prove to them who the true God was. "If the Lord be God, follow Him; but if Baal, then follow him." (1 Kings 18:21) As you recall, the pagan priests and prophets danced, wailed and cried all night long for their god to show his strength. But nothing happened. Then Elijah got up, called on the Name of the Lord and "fire immediately came down from heaven and consumed his offering." (1 Kings 18:38)

Elijah then slew the false prophets and was given supernatural strength to outrun King Ahab's chariot back to the city. As Scripture puts it, "The hand of the Lord was [mightily] upon Elijah." (1 Kings 18:46) I certainly would say it was! But when King Ahab told his wife Jezebel all that Elijah had done, she was furious and sent a message back to him, threatening his life. This letter made Elijah deathly afraid and he fled for his life. Jezebel spoke as an enemy who might say, "You've had it; you've gone too far. *The battle is now between you and me.*" (1 Kings 19:2)

The interesting part about this statement is that it was the truth! The battle on Mount Carmel was *not* between Elijah and the prophets of Baal, but between good and evil, the Lord and the devil. It *was* a battle between the powers of darkness and God's body of believers here on earth ("light bearers"). Queen Jezebel represented Satan and his demon hordes as his tool to bring disorder, confusion and turmoil. Elijah represented the Lord and His believers.

As a result of that vicious threat from Jezebel, Elijah sat down outside the city gates, filled with fear and spiritual pride. He wailed to himself, "Only I am left. All the others have been slain and now they seek my life." (1 Kings 19:10) He continued to accuse the Lord, in effect saying, "God, you let the devil get to me. You let him harass me. You let him take away my joy. I don't deserve such treatment. I have done everything you told me to. After all I've done, I end up with the biggest battle of my life."

This is the mighty prophet that just slew 750 prophets of Baal! Can you believe it? Is it any wonder then, that we too have our down days when the enemy's taunts consume us? As a result of Elijah's self-consumed thinking, he panicked, feared for his life, became depressed and eventually, prayed to die. (1 Kings 19:4)

Jezebel Today

I want you to really think about this story, because this is exactly what's happening to many believers today. Jezebel represents Satan in the story of Elijah. She was his tool to bring confusion, disorder and turmoil into Elijah's life. And it almost worked. Well, the spirit of Jezebel is back in these end times and she is trying to do the exact same thing in our lives. When we determine to surrender and live totally for God and learn to worship Him, she uses the same tactics she used with Elijah. She wants to break our will and our spirit.

God warns us when in Revelation 2:19-22, He speaks to the end-time Church of Thyatira, "...I know thy works, and charity, and service, and faith, and thy patience, and thy works; and the last to be more than the first. *Notwithstanding I have a few things against thee, because thou sufferest that woman Jezebel, which calleth herself a prophetess, to teach and to seduce my servants...*"

I believe Jezebel represents a seducing spirit that is at work among worshipers in these end times, just as this Scripture says. Her goal is to rob us of our desire to serve the Lord, and to quench our hope in God's faithfulness, tactics just like those with Elijah. If the spirit of Jezebel can make us think that God's Word is not true and that He is not faithful to perform what God promises, then our relationship with the Lord will immediately collapse.

If the spirit of Jezebel can undermine our confidence in the Lord, she has us. The truth is, the Lord values His Word even above His Name. Thus, if He promises something in His Word, He will perform it no matter what.

Psalm 138:2 validates this: " I will worship toward Thy holy temple, and praise Thy Name for Thy lovingkindness and for Thy truth: *for Thou hast magnified Thy Word above all Thy Name.*"

Jezebel wants to side-track us: from worshiping, to worrying; from being on fire for the Lord, to being lukewarm; and from loving Him, to doubting Him. She wants us caught up in the "Oh, poor me" syndrome, filled with self-pity and spiraling straight down into the pit.

When we begin to truly worship, entering His presence daily, vocally sharing our faith and acting as Christ would, then watch out! The spirit of Jezebel will use our loved ones, any situations she can create and, any lies, fears, depression or confusion she can prompt, expressly to take control of our lives. Now when I say "take control," I don't mean "possession." If we are born again, then our heart and our spirit already belong to the Lord. But if we give the enemy "entrances" into our soul by doubt, unbelief and confusion, she will use them to her full advantage. The spirit of Jezebel did it with Elijah. She will do it with us.

It's one thing to stand up for Christ with our friends, our family and our co-workers, but it's quite another to stand up against the forces of darkness.

Let's see what we can glean from Elijah's experience.

Lessons From the Story of Elijah

There are many lessons we can learn from the story of Elijah. Here are just a few:

1) Even if we run, God is still with us. (1 Kings 19:5-8)
2) In order for us to really battle Satan, we must know his reality.
3) In order to regain control, we must unmask the enemy's game plan. When we begin to understand what Jezebel is up to, we can begin our walk back to freedom. Fear is what keeps us captive. It did Elijah and it will us also. (1 Kings 19:12-18)
4) Satan wants to use our thoughts, our emotions, our circumstances and our relationships to destroy us; God wants to use them to strengthen our faith. (Psalm 71)
5) We must listen to God's voice (1 King's 19:12) and take back control of our lives. When the Lord says: *Why are you hiding,* we must heed His call. When He says, *Get up, don't run from Jezebel,* we must obey.

Once Elijah realized what Jezebel was doing, he never again allowed her to capture his mind.

Whether we admit it or not, we are in an intense battle. God knows that if we are not "battle-ready," He can't commission us into the heavy artillery. (Jeremiah 12:5) In other words, if we are wearied in any way by the enemy, God knows that we'll *never* make it through the really tough times ahead. Thus, we have no other choice. Either we learn to fight as God desires, or we'll end up like Elijah, cowering in a corner.

Spirit of Jezebel

Satan's main targets today are people in leadership, those totally surrendered to the Lord and true worshipers. The spirit of Jezebel is looking for total "control" in our lives. Now, again, I'm not talking about "possession," because these are Christians, but simply mental and emotional confusion, doubt, manipulation, depression, discouragement, despair, etc. By allowing these kinds of things into our souls, we leave the door wide open for the enemy. Again, look at Elijah's example.

The spirit of Jezebel seems to attack through three main areas: discouragement, confusion and depression. The enemy has set up his own cycle of defeat for us and it goes something like this: *discouragement* leads to confusion; *confusion* leads to depression; *depression* leads to loss of vision; *loss of vision* leads to disorientation; *disorientation* leads to withdrawal; *withdrawal* leads to despair; and *despair* leads to *defeat.*[17]

---

[17] From Francis Frangipane's book, *The Jezebel Spirit.*.

It's so true. Each one of these areas leads us right down the ladder to the next, until you find yourself caught in a web so thick that there's no way out. Watch out for this in your own life. Recognize it. Then, make the faith choices you need to, back to freedom.

As we said earlier, the people we know and love the most, are often the ones who hurt us the most. They do so through "control" and "manipulation". And, if we allow bitterness or resentment to result, the enemy will have entrapped us also. In other words, the negative emotions which result from our resistance can often become a trap the enemy sets for us. The devil wins whenever he can get us to react to any spirit other than the Holy Spirit. (Galatians 5:22-23)

The spirit of Jezebel wants us to depart from the fruit of the Spirit to the poison of self. And she delights when we try to combat other's actions in our own strength. Bitterness, resentment, etc., will never cast Jezebel out but only increase her powers.

The only antidote is repentance, love and warfare.

Unfortunately, everyone in ministry will at some point endure a form of rejection and misunderstanding. Now, some of these Christians will be able to handle it in a godly manner and deal with it as God would have them. Others, however, when they realize they cannot control the situation, will reject the people involved.

Remember the story of David with King Saul. When Saul realized he couldn't control David, he not only ended up resenting and being jealous of him, but also he tried to physically harm him. (1 Samuel 24)

When we rebel against the Holy Spirit and don't deal with our sinful thoughts and emotions as God would have us (as we learned in Chapter Three), that void is often filled by the spirit of Jezebel. Depression, confusion and fear are just the entrance she is waiting for. Then, we'll find ourselves falling down the "cycle of defeat," just like Elijah.

What the Enemy Fears

What the enemy fears the most is repentance. As we saw in earlier chapters, repentance is the key to a surrendered, spirit-filled life and Jezebel knows this. It's interesting that Elijah is the very one who represented "the call to repentance." He exhorted Israel to return to God and to raise up true warring and worshiping prophets. Because he tried to accomplish this in his own power and ability, however, even after his great victory on Mt. Carmel, he slipped into the flesh and fell. He forgot that all authority gained by our own efforts will simply become a stumbling block to receiving true authority from God. Thus, as seen in his own life, it can become an entrance for the enemy.

True spirituality is measured by displaying Christ's meekness and His humility, not by our own control and power. *We must seek humility before position.* Otherwise, we open ourselves up to the enemy. All self-seeking, self-promotion, self-preservation and self-centeredness must be destroyed and our focus returned to Christ-likeness. God's way is to "use" the weakest of us—"the foolish things of the world,"—fill us with Himself and then, exalt us to the highest position.

When we depend upon our own strength and our own power to accomplish God's will, we give room to the spirit of Jezebel. The antidote to this is to refuse to take any authority or any influence in our own power and strength, and instead, *rely completely upon the Lord to establish us.* This is why those in leadership are such prime targets for the deceptions and tricks of the spirit of Jezebel. The temptation is always there to take matters into our own hands and somehow, "make them work." As 1 Peter 5:6 says, "Humble yourselves therefore under the mighty hand of God, [so] that He may exalt you in due time."

King David is a great example of this. During his reign, with the exception of the episode with Bathsheba, *he refused to lift a hand to seek his own recognition or his own influence.* And, as a result, the New Testament tells us that David was known as "a man after God's own heart." (Acts 13:22) Even in the situation with

Saul, David never took matters into his own hands, but insisted upon always exposing his own personal motives, and trusting God with the outcome of the situation. (1 Samuel 24:10) In other words, he demonstrated the exact opposite of a controlling spirit. This, unfortunately, is *not* the norm in today's churches and probably one of the major *root* causes for much of the division we experience.

The Answer

As we have said before, the answer to the enemy's tactics of pride, control, insecurity, fear, etc., is *surrender, repentance* and *love*. We must quit following our own ways, choose to turn around and follow God. And, we must constantly ask God to expose our efforts to control or manipulate others or situations. And, when He does so, we mustn't collapse in guilt and remorse over these things, allowing more strongholds for the enemy, but simply confess, choose to turn around and give everything to the Lord.

Trying to take control of situations or of others is, unfortunately, one of the first ways our "flesh" rears its ugly head. As we know, the flesh is continuously warring against the spirit, but through confession and repentance, it *can* be overcome. *God's way always leads us back to the Cross.*

Unless we can see the situation through God's eyes and through His Love, we will *not* be seeing clearly at all. In other words, any insecurity, any self-preservation, any self-promotion, unhealed wounds, unforgiveness or bitterness will neutralize our discernment and destroy our ability to walk by the Spirit. We won't be able to interpret our circumstances accurately. True spiritual discernment only comes to light through worship and intimacy with the Lord. Matthew 5:44 tells us, "We are to bless those that curse us, and pray for those who despitefully use us." *By grace, we can choose to lay our lives down for one another.* We can't be holy without total obedience to God's command to love one another.

"Repentance and forgiveness" simply means the freedom not to reciprocate from our wounds and hurts, but from Christ's Life within. This is the only response that causes the evil spirit to flee.

Paul in the New Testament experienced such horrific attacks from the enemy that he even despaired of life itself. His answer, however, was not to give up and die, but to repent and trust God even more. Listen to 2 Corinthians 1:9, "...we have the sentence of death in ourselves, that we should not trust in ourselves, but in God which raiseth the dead."

And we must determine to do the same. Never give in to doubt and strife, but simply have deeper faith in God's unfathomable ways, trusting that He will lead us in His perfect way. (John 10:27) Isaiah 30:21 tells it this way, "And thine ears shall hear a word behind thee, saying, This *is* the way, walk ye in it..." Again, we are not required to understand all that He does, but simply to trust Him *in* all that He does.

Keys to the Kingdom

Jesus gives us *the answer* to all of this in Matthew 16:19. He calls it the "keys" to the kingdom. "I will give unto thee the keys of the kingdom of heaven: and whatsoever thou shalt *bind* on earth shall be bound in heaven: and whatsoever thou shalt *loose* on earth shall be loosed in heaven."

I've been a Christian for over 45 years and always understood the terms "binding and loosing" to mean *binding the enemy* and *loosing the Holy Spirit.* However, after reading and studying several books lately on the subject, I've come to see that there are actually two ways of looking at this verse. Now please understand, I am not a theologian, nor a scholar, so you check out everything I say.

The word *to bind* actually means "to be in bonds, to be tied up, to yoke, to harness, to knit or to join together; to make ready or to prepare." Whereas, the word *to loose* means "to break up, to dissolve, to unloose or melt away." Binding and loosing are Hebrew idioms for exercising power and authority. These, Jesus says, are the "keys" to the kingdom.

We mentioned earlier that Jesus is our example. It's very interesting because Jesus *never* "bound the enemy" or "loosed the Spirit." What He did was simply rebuke the enemy, command him to flee, and pray for the Spirit of God to take over. Thus, another way of looking at the term "to loose," is that we have Jesus' authority and His power to loose, pull down and crucify any stronghold in our old nature. A stronghold is a fortified hideout or a walled defense of the enemy, which needs to be exposed, broken up and dissolved.

For example, feelings of resentment can lead to the stronghold of bitterness; confusion can lead to the stronghold of discouragement; and feelings of betrayal can lead to distrust. These negative thoughts and feelings are often protected by self-erected strongholds (fortified walled defenses that keep out more pain). We often depend upon these strongholds to protect our right to believe something. Unfortunately, these defenses can also make comfortable hideouts and camps for the enemy. Thus, the Lord wants these strongholds *loosed,* broken up and dissolved.

Another way of looking at the term *to bind* is to see that it also can mean "to join together" like a parent binding his child to himself. Somewhat like strapping a baby pack on your back. In other words, we bind ourselves to the Lord when we "join" our will to His will, our thoughts to His thoughts, our mind to His mind, etc. Philippians 2:5 tells us, "Let this mind be in you, which was also in Christ Jesus..."

Consequently, by the authority and power that Christ has given us as His children, we can *loose the strongholds of our old nature*—"the bands of wickedness" (Isaiah 58:6), and then we can bind ourselves to the Lord, His will, His mind and His truth. When we yoke and harness ourselves to the Lord, we destroy, dissolve, break apart, crush or smash any deception around which the strongholds are built.

The only way we are ever going to be conformed into Christ's image is by surrendering every stronghold, every emotion, every thought, every desire, every attitude, every fear, inside and out, that might create opportunities for the enemy. There's a huge difference between simply *defining the sin* and actually *pulling down the strongholds* that helped produce it. This, to me, is what God is trying to teach us by "binding and loosing." It's also what Satan is trying to prevent at all costs.

As Matthew tells us, the "key" to spiritual warfare is understanding and implementing these terms.

Part of our worship time, therefore, should be binding ourselves to Lord, thus stabilizing our mind, will and emotions. *Next*, praying and asking the Lord to loose any strongholds—any bands of wickedness, any self-protective defense mechanisms—that have been layered over by any of our unmet needs and have, thus, hindered our walk with Him. And, *finally*, in the Name of Jesus Christ, commanding Satan and his spirit of Jezebel to be gone—to go to the pit of hell where they belong. Recently, I've gotten a little bolder and have begun to pray that the Lord annihilate, eradicate and vaporize every demonic spirit trying to kill, steal and destroy the works of God. Scripture tells us that we have the power and authority of Jesus Christ to do this—because we belong to Him.

One of these Scriptures is Matthew 10:1, "And when He had called unto Him His twelve disciples, He gave them power against unclean spirits, to cast them out..." I also like Psalm 149:8 which says, "Bind their kings with chains." Let's bind the enemy with chains and then command him, in Jesus Christ's Name, to be gone, exterminated and obliterated. (Zechariah 3:2)

This binding, loosing and commanding (the enemy to be gone) in the Name, authority and power of Christ, must go alongside of worshiping the Lord. If we don't learn how to do this, it would be analogous to taking off our grave clothes, but *not* rolling away the stone. (Isaiah 37:3)

Warfare Prayer

If you are like me, when you pray (and especially, if it's a new prayer), it's always helpful to have an rough example to follow. Yes, the Holy Spirit must always lead, but it's nice to have a guideline when you are just beginning. So, here is an idea of how you might begin to pray. But if this doesn't meet your needs, then, by all means, let the Holy Spirit write your own.

"Father, as a child of God, You have given me Your power and Your authority to rebuke the enemy and to cast him out. You tell us that "greater is He that is in us, than he who is in the world." (1 John 4:4)

I ask You now to part the heavens and come down! Mount the cherubim and fly! Soar on the wings of the wind! Shoot Your arrows at the enemy and scatter him to the outermost parts. (Psalm 18 paraphrased)

In Your Name and with the authority that You have given me, I ask You to *loose* any strongholds in me where the enemy might be hiding out—any root of bitterness, unforgiveness or resentment. I ask You to command Satan, all his hordes of demons and his spirit of Jezebel, to be gone in the Name and power of Jesus Christ. I ask You to cast them out to the outermost parts, there to be annihilated, eradicated and vaporized.

I ask for the Blood of Christ to cover me, protect me and prevent the enemy from returning. I *bind* my will, my thoughts and my life to You. I love You, Lord, my Deliverer. Thank You for rescuing me and for bringing me to a safe place. Amen.

Warfare Scripture Prayers

Some further Scriptures that arm us (and, again, be Spirit-led) in our spiritual warfare are:

Peter 5:8-9 - Resist the devil (who is a roaring lion) knowing that all Christians are in the same battle. You promise us, God, that after we have "barred ourselves from sin," You will make us perfect, established and strengthened.

James 4:7-10 - Submit ourselves to God (go through *The Inner Court Ritual*), resist the devil and he will flee from us. Draw close to God and He will draw close to us. Cleanse our hands (body) and purify our hearts (spirit). Humble ourselves in the sight of God and He will lift us up.

Revelation 12:11 - The way we overcome the enemy is by the blood of Christ, the Word of our testimony and by "death to self."

1 John 4:4 - Greater is He that is in us (Jesus) than he that is in the world. Even the spirits are subject to us. (Also Luke 10:20)

Psalm 144:1 - Blessed be God, who teaches my hands to war. (Also Psalm 18:34)

Psalm 149:6 – Let the high praises of God be in their mouth, and a two-edged sword in their hand.

Deliverance Prayers

The following are some Scriptures to pray for deliverance. Again, depend completely upon the Holy Spirit for direction.   (I have taken the liberty to paraphrase these Scriptures):

Hebrews 4:16 - I come boldly before Your throne in time of need.
Romans 8:26 - The Spirit knows how to pray.
2 Corinthians 4:4 - The god of this world has blinded the eyes of those who don't believe.
2 Corinthians 2:10-11 - We must forgive so that Satan doesn't get an advantage in us.
Luke 10:19 - You (Jesus) give us the authority over the power of the enemy so that nothing shall hurt us.
Galatians 1:4 - You deliver us from this present evil world.
Colossians 1:13 - You have delivered us from the authority of darkness.

2 Timothy 2:25-26 - God, give repentance to the acknowledging of the truth, so that they may recover
from the snare of the evil one.

1 John 3:8 - You were manifested to destroy the works
of the devil.

2 Chronicles 20:15 - Be not afraid, the battle is not
ours, but God's.

Colossians 2:15 - God has defeated principalities and
powers.

Matthew 12:29 - How can we enter a strong man's house
(the enemy's house), unless we first bind him (see
Psalm 149:8), and then we can spoil his goods.

Psalm 149:6-8 - Let the high praises of God be in our
mouths, and a two-edged sword in our hands, and
may You (Jesus) bind the enemy's kings with chains.

Armor of God Prayers

Further spiritual warfare prayers that we can pray are:

Ephesians 6:10-19 exhorts us to daily put on the
"armor of God." Then, we will be strong in the power
of *His* might and be able to withstand the wiles of the
enemy:

Having girt our waist with God's Truth.

Putting on the **Breastplate of Righteousness** and
Love. (1 Thessalonians 5:8)

Having shod our feet (our soul) with the **Gospel of Peace**. (Putting off the "flesh" and putting on Christ is how we wash our feet.)

Taking the **Shield of Faith** by which we can quench the fiery darts. (This is one of the most important parts of our armor because it's our choice to trust what God has promised us in His Word.)

The **Helmet of Salvation**. (This is the showing forth of God's Life instead of our own. It's His light that is shining forth. As Isaiah 62:1 says, "Salvation [is] a lamp that burneth.")

The **Sword of the Spirit** which is the Word of God. [The Word of God is our "battle ax" and the only way we are able to stand. (Jeremiah 51:20)]

Praying always for all the saints. (We are to be constantly praying to God on behalf of all the saints.)

That utterance may be given to us to make known the **mystery of the Gospel** (in everything we say and do).

Just as the priests, once they had finished worshiping at the Incense Altar, came out to the people and blessed them and taught them, so we too can do the same. We can share of the fulness of the Lord that we have received while in His presence.

Chapter Six
Questions

1) What does "spiritual warfare" have to do with *worshiping God*?

2) When we are "lukewarm" for Christ, the enemy doesn't seem to bother with us very much. Why? Why are we such *targets* when we begin to worship and live for the Lord? (John 16:2)

3) Why is *surrendering* the key to fighting the enemy? Give some Scriptural examples of men or women who were surrendered and victorious. How did they do it? (Acts 7:59; Job 13:15; 2 Corinthians 1:8)

4) Write out 2 Corinthians 4:8-9 and explain what this Scripture really means.

5) Why does God allow such horrific things into our lives? (Deuteronomy 8:2) Why is it so important to have strong faith? (Jeremiah 12:5) What is the key to a strong faith?

6) Why is the story of Elijah so appropriate for to-day? What are some of the lessons we learn from it? (1 Kings 19:5-8, 12-18) Who does Elijah represent? Jezebel? Why?

7) Why did Elijah flee? (1 Kings 19:4) Have you ever felt the same way?

8) What was Jezebel's mission in Elijah's life? In like manner, what is she trying to do in believer's lives today? Do you see a parallel today?

9) What is the spirit of Jezebel after in our lives? Name the "cycle of defeat" she has planned for every worshiping Christian? Have you experienced any of these things in your own life?

10) When we respond to other's sin with bitterness and resentment, what does this do for Jezebel? What are the three elements necessary *in us* for subduing Jezebel? (John 10:27; Isaiah 30:21)

11) What is it that Satan and his spirit of Jezebel fear the most? (1 Peter 5:6) Give a Scriptural example of this? (1 Samuel 24)

12) Matthew 16:19 tells us that *binding and loosing* in Jesus' name are the "keys to the kingdom." Explain what this means to you. What is another way of looking at the terms *binding* and *loosing*?

Private Worship -
The Key to Joy

The Fulness of His Joy

Joy is said to take possession of our whole man. This means that when we are "in the presence of the Lord," we will be filled from head to toe with unspeakable joy. (Nehemiah 8:10) And this joy is what gives us the strength to withstand whatever circumstances the Lord may allow into our lives. As Paul expresses it, "I am *exceedingly joyful* in all [my] tribulation." (2 Corinthians 7:4) In other words, he is so full of joy from being in the Lord's presence that it doesn't matter what his circumstances are. This is an astounding statement in light of the horrific trials and problems that Paul faced.

Worship is the key to this kind of joy, simply because worship is the key to the Lord's presence. Again, Psalm 16:11, "Thou wilt shew me the path of life: *in Thy presence is fullness of joy* and at Thy right hand there are pleasures forevermore."

Remember Mary and how she laid before the Lord, continually washing and bathing His feet with her tears. Mary was worshiping the Lord from the depth of her being, totally consumed in her love for Him and overwhelmed by the inner joy she was experiencing. She wasn't aware of anything else at that moment, because Jesus was her complete focus. She was one with her Lord and full of His joy.

Jesus tells us in John 15:10-11, "If ye keep my commandments, ye shall abide in My Love even as I have kept my Father's commandments, and abide in His Love. These things have I spoken unto you, that My joy might remain in you and *that your joy may be full* [or complete]." Jesus had perfect joy because He always did the Father's will and was in constant communion with Him. Consequently, as we do the Father's will (surrender, love and worship Him), and as we commune with Him, our joy will also be complete.

Isaiah 56:7 confirms this, "Even them will I bring to My holy mountain, and make them joyful in My house of prayer: their burnt offerings and their sacrifices *shall be* accepted upon Mine altar; for Mine house shall be called an house of prayer for all people."

Restoring the Joy of our Salvation

Now, there is a type of joy that occurs when we first become believers and it's wonderful and lasts for awhile. But, once our circumstances become more difficult, this type of joy often disappears. The kind of joy that we 've been talking about throughout this book, *the joy of our salvation,* does *not* come from our circumstances, but is a gift directly from the Lord. This type of unspeakable joy comes only as a result of being before Him in worship. (Psalm 9:14; 21:1) And, thus, this type of joy will not diminish if our circumstances take a turn for the worse.

Let me give you a recent example: This past December, the Lord prompted us to expand our ministry and establish *The King's Place.* This is the local outreach of *The King's High Way Ministries* and *Koinonia House.* It's a Christian crisis center focusing on teaching, discipling and encouraging those who are undergoing marriage struggles, drug abuse problems, alcoholism, etc.

We found a little house in downtown Coeur d'Alene that was absolutely perfect. It had great visibility (on a busy downtown street), wonderful accessibility (you could walk everywhere), and yet was homey and comfortable. We didn't want to minister to hurting people out of a cold and impersonal business office. We wanted a safe, home environment. The little house we found was just right and we knew it was God's choice. So, we moved in February 4th—computers, desks, phones, etc., etc.

There was, however, one small problem. The property needed to be re-zoned: it still was zoned "residential" and needed to be changed to "commercial," in order that we could have classes and sell the *King's High Way* materials. "No problem," we were told. Across the street the zoning is already commercial; the other end of our same block is, also; and behind us there are already multiple dwellings. So, we thought, no problem! It's a shoe-in!

Wrong!

The Planning Commission turned us down 6 to 0! We were absolutely shocked! We couldn't believe it! Nobody could believe it. It meant we had to move.

I went home that night, fell on my face and began to worship the Lord, pouring my heart out before Him. What happened next was unbelievable. I could not contain the joy that began to flow from my being. I have never experienced anything like it. Here it was, one of the worst days of my life, and yet I am overflowing with joy. It was totally supernatural! It reminded me of Paul's words, "I am exceedingly joyful in all my tribulation." (2 Corinthians 7:4) God began to speak to my heart that this *was* our ministry home and I was not to worry. *He had "other things" in mind besides "zone changes."* He wanted to use this difficult situation to change many hearts.

And this is exactly what has happened. We made another modified application, and we have watched in utter amazement as many people at City Hall have become acquainted with the ministry and touched by God's Love. Several have even commented, "We're rooting for you." Our neighbors, who didn't know who we were the first time around, all know us now by our first names and have allowed us into their hearts and to pray for their personal circumstances. The gentleman who stood up and spoke *against* us at the last meeting, now calls us regularly. His wife and I have gone to lunch, and he even stood up and spoke *for us* in the latest hearing. Our landlord has been absolutely stupefied as he has watched God perform miracles in the situation. He commented last week, "Boy, it's not how I would have tackled the problem (he was angry and wanted to get even), but, man, it's certainly *a much better way!*" He let us give him a Bible and is now listening to audio tapes on the same. Our architect, who will be building the classrooms for us, has been amazed at how things have worked out.

So, we again went before the Planning Commission and were approved 6 to 0. Ten people stood up and spoke on our behalf, including our neighbor who "changed his mind" and now wanted the King's Place. Another gentleman who spoke on our behalf flew all the way from New Zealand to do so! You could see the men and women on the Planning Commission panel soften, change, and then become excited about our vision. It's an absolute miracle! (Earlier in the day we had been told by a friend of the mayor that he didn't believe we had a chance!)

But, with God "all things *are* possible"!

"For My thoughts are not your thoughts, neither are your ways my ways, saith the Lord. For as the heavens are higher than the earth, so are My ways higher than your ways, and My thoughts than your thoughts." (Isaiah 55:8-9)

God always has much bigger things in mind than our little "circumstances." And even though His ways of accomplishing His will in our lives are not always our ways, His ways are always much better.

This kind of supernatural joy does not come from our circumstances, our emotions or others' actions, but is purely a gift from the Lord—it's the joy of our salvation.

1 Peter 1:8 expresses it perfectly: "Whom having not seen, ye love; in whom, though now ye see Him not, yet believing, ye rejoice with joy unspeakable and full of glory."

Again, this kind of joy is always associated with God's presence.

Joy Instead of Mourning

Learning to worship the Lord on a daily basis does not preclude our having more trials and temptations, unfortunately, but actually necessitates it. In other words, experiencing deeper consecration requires even more refining. Our crown is only gained through the cross. So, we will be treated just as the Father did with Jesus. First, He was visibly and audibly approved of, "This is my beloved Son in whom I am well pleased." (Matthew 3:17) Then, after that glorious beginning, Jesus was led into the wilderness for 40 days and 40 nights to be tempted of the devil. (Matthew 4:1-2; Mark 1:12-13; Luke 4:1-13)

Moses is another example of one who was first exalted, and then abased. Moses was with the Lord for 40 days and 40 nights on the mountain (Exodus 3), experiencing things that no other human being has ever seen or touched. But after that incredible encounter, he too sustained even more horrific attacks through Pharaoh and others.

Finally, there was Elijah, who also saw miraculous events from the Lord, but shortly afterwards, holed himself up in a cave and experienced terrifying things. And, of course, there are many others in Scripture who underwent the same kind of pattern. (Jonah, Abraham, Jacob, David, Paul, etc.)

Thus, there seems to be a close connection between being initially crowned with the Holy Spirit and filled with joy at His presence and being tormented and accused by the enemy.

According to the Bible, sorrow often is the means by which God enlarges our capacity for joy. In other words, God uses persecution to enhance our happiness.

John 16:20-22 validates this, "Verily, verily, I say unto you, That ye shall weep and lament, but the world shall rejoice: and ye shall be sorrowful, but your sorrow shall be turned into joy. A woman when she is in travail hath sorrow, because her hour is come: but as soon as she is delivered of the child, she remembereth no more the anguish, for joy that a man is born into the world. And ye now therefore have sorrow: but I will see you again, and your heart shall rejoice, and your joy no man taketh from you." See also 2 Corinthians 4:8-9; Acts 5:41; Romans 5:3; 2 Corinthians 8:2; James 1:2.

When at the depths of a trial, if we can respond in such a way that the situation pushes us into God's presence, then we can expect to experience the joy of the Lord in spite of our circumstances. Faith choices to worship the Lord in the midst of our difficulties will bring us His unspeakable joy. In 2 Corinthians 7:4, Paul simply tells us, "I am exceeding joyful in all [my] tribulation." See also Philippians 4:4. And this is what will get us through.

Path to Victory

The pattern is clear: first, we are approved of by God; then we are tempted by many trials and tribulations; and finally, we receive our crown. If we know how to enter the Lord's presence and worship Him in the midst of our suffering, then we will receive "beauty for our ashes" and the "oil of joy instead of mourning." (Isaiah 61:3)

Now more than ever before however, we need to sanctify the Lord in the eyes of others. This simply means rejoicing in the middle of our trials, so that Jesus will be glorified. God's Word promises that Jesus will never leave us nor forsake us, but will be at our right hand helping us through and bringing us to victory. If we really believe this, then we must walk it out. In other words, we must show others by our actions what we believe. Our only responsibility is to trust the Lord enough during our trials to demonstrate His Life through us.

David Wilkerson comments on this in one of his recent newsletters. He says that no matter where we are in our walk with the Lord, we must "make a joyful noise unto Him." (Psalm 66:1; 98:4-6)   He says if we don't, "the very stones [themselves] will cry out." (Luke 19:40)

Humility

The essence of worship, then, is really self-abasement and humility. This does not mean putting ourselves down in a self-condemning way, but simply *not thinking about ourselves at all.* Humility is the ability to see ourselves as we truly are, which then leaves us free to get excited about the triumphs of others and love as God desires.

Humility is putting Christ and what He wants first. It's putting away all self-seeking, self-promotion and self-preservation. We are to exalt Christ and Him alone. *Humility, thus, is the mark of a true worshiper.*

If you take a look at some of the people in the Bible whom the Lord used in magnificent ways (Noah, Moses, Peter, Joseph, David, etc.), you will find a common thread among them. He often chose the weakest and the lowliest of men. And this is still true today. God's standard of spirituality is measured by *meekness*, not power. Of course, the world and the devil try to constantly whisper otherwise, but always meekness and humility foil their plans.

The Glory of God

Throughout Scripture, we see God's pattern of abasement and then exultation. John 12:24, "Verily, verily, I say unto you, Except a corn of wheat fall into the ground and die, it abideth alone: but if it die, it bringeth forth much fruit." Look at the lives of Moses, Joseph, Paul, Peter, etc. In Revelation, God promises that those who "overcome" the world, the flesh and the devil, will inherit *the morning star*. (Revelation 2:26-28) This simply represents Christ's visible outward glory, which is a symbol of His hidden inward purity.

Remember the story of Moses in Exodus 34:33-34. His encounter with the Lord on Mount Sinai so radically changed him that his face shone with the glory of God. *Glory is the result of being in the Lord's presence.* We not only receive fulness of joy from being before Him, but also His glory will be reflected through our countenance. Scripture validates this, "Those who look to Him for help will be radiant." (Psalm 34:5 Living Translation)

Paul talks about this in Galatians 1:15-16, when he says that God called him from birth to "reveal [or to glorify] His Son" in him. Paul is saying here that as Jesus becomes our life itself, when others look at us, they will see Christ's reflection, just as they did with Moses. We will reflect His image.

A person's countenance is the outward expression of what is in his heart. Moses simply reflected *externally* the glory of God that he was experiencing *internally*. And the same experience can be true of us also. The more we are with the Lord, the more of His glory we will reflect.

Jesus is the full revelation of God's glory and if He abides in us, that glory is going to shine forth in our lives also. Jesus wants to express His glory *through us*. We are His arms and legs. Now, others might not see our face shining as they did Moses, but they should, at least, see something in our countenance that reflects Christ's character.

It's interesting because the very first time Moses saw God's glory, was the first time he worshiped Him. (Exodus 34:6-8) Thus, there is a connection between the revelation of His glory and worshiping Him. Experiencing God's glory not only changes us—from glory to glory—it also changes our worship of Him.

In the temple, the place where God's glory was manifested was at the Incense Altar, which sat directly before the Mercy Seat. As we said earlier, this altar was considered to be a part of the Holy of Holies, but actually stood in the Holy Place. It was called "the altar before the Lord." (Revelation 8:3) After the incense was offered, the Shekinah Glory would come forth from the Holy of Holies, co-mingle with the perfumed cloud of incense, and then arise and fill the temple. The priest would then fall on his face and worship the Lord.

This is a visual picture of what happens when we humble ourselves and worship the Lord at the Incense Altar of our hearts. We not only become one spirit with Him, but the glory of God fills the temple of our body. In the perilous times ahead, Scripture tells us that God's glory will be our defense, our covering and our protection. His glory will shelter us from the intense trouble that is to come upon the earth. Once again, God will put His pillar of cloud and fire over His Church for comfort and for direction. "The Lord will create upon every dwelling place of Mount Zion and upon her assemblies, a cloud and smoke by day, and the shining of a flaming fire by night; for upon all the glory shall be a defense." (Isaiah 4:5-6)

Walking with the Lord

Worship involves companionship, communion, fellowship, mutual delight and decision making. These are the things that build a firm foundation so that we are able to "walk with the Lord," share His heart and enjoy Him as a friend.

Abel, Enoch, Noah and Abraham all "walked with the Lord." (Genesis 5:22; 6:9) Each humbly sought His presence and the Lord rewarded them by revealing His glory.

Scripture says that Enoch never performed anything spectacular or noteworthy. Yet, the Word tells us that "he walked with God." Likewise, Noah found grace in the eyes of the Lord and thus, the Lord shared His heart with Him. And, of course, Scripture records that Abraham was the Lord's "friend". (James 2:23; Isaiah 41:8) As David Wilkerson puts it, "to have the Creator of the Universe call you His friend seems almost beyond human comprehension."

Worship is the only place that a firm foundation for a "walking relationship" can be built. As Bob Sorge says, "We must develop a secret history with God *before* He gives us a public one."

Conclusion

In conclusion, if you have identified with some of the things that have been shared in this book: if you, too, have lost the joy of your salvation; if you, too, have never really understood what true "worship" is; and if you, too, have longed to be consumed in God's Love and His presence, then I urge you to put into practice what it means to personally worship the Lord. I assure you it will change your life and become the most important part of your entire day.

I now understand what Psalm 65:4 means when it says, "Blessed is the man whom Thou choosest and causeth to approach unto Thee; that he may dwell in Thy courts..." or, as the Living Translation says, "What joy awaits us inside Your Holy Temple!" The Lord is waiting there to give us the "oil of joy" and the "glory of His presence." (Isaiah 61:3) *Worship is the key to experiencing His presence, to knowing the indescribable joy of our salvation, and to reflecting His glory.* Isaiah 56:7 tells us that the Lord will, "Bring us to His holy mountain and make us joyful..." Or as the Living translation says, "Fill [us] with joy in [His] house of prayer."

When we worship, we are not only loving God, but He is loving us in return. Communion is *giving,* as well as *receiving.* We give the Lord our worship and our love. He then gives us His joy, His glory and, of course, His Love. Worship flows from our love of Him; joy and glory come from His Love towards us.

Thus, regardless of what is going on in our lives, if we choose to humble ourselves, worship and adore Him, *He will align our feelings with our faith choices, make His presence known, and, then, fill us with His joy.* (Psalm 71) This is what gives us *hope*—hope that He still cares and that He is intimately concerned about every single detail of our lives.

The greatest experience the world has to offer is human love and, of course, it's expression in the sexual act. The world tells us that *this* is what will bring us "happiness" and fulfilment. Consequently, everyone is running around frantically searching for this "ultimate experience."

Now, human love is wonderful and for those of us fortunate enough to have experienced it, it *is* euphoric and it is great. *But, this in itself does not bring us happiness, joy or fulfilment!* Look at all the people in the world who are known to have had phenomenal and public love affairs, innumerable sexual encounters and multiple marriages, but many of whom are *still* unfulfilled and still searching. Did that ultimate expression of worldly love bring them happiness? Apparently not! They're still looking for it!

The Creator of the Universe, the One who designed us in the first place, has planned something far greater for those who seek Him with all their hearts. He tells us that *only in His presence is true happiness; only in His presence is complete fulfilment; and only in His presence is fulness of joy.* (And, we don't have to wait until we get to heaven in order to taste this.)

By learning to worship Him in the Spirit–not just on Sundays in church, but privately at home–every day, we will be able to experience the fulfilment and the joy that the world and everyone in it is so desperately searching for, *but very few seem to have found.*

Truly, private Worship is̲ the Key to Joy and Happiness!

"Thou hast made known to me the ways of life; Thou shalt make me full of joy with thy countenance."

Acts 2:28

Chapter Seven
Questions

1) Psalm 16:11 tells us that when we are in the presence of the Lord, we will be filled with unspeakable joy. Why? What occurs that makes us so joyful?

2) How is the joy of our salvation different from the joy that comes from our circumstances? (1 Peter 1:8; Psalm 9:14)

3) Will all our trials cease when we learn to truly worship the Lord? Why/why not? Give some Scriptural examples. How about some personal examples?

4) What is the pattern that God often works into our lives *before* we receive our crowns? (John 16:22; Isaiah 61:3)

5) What does it mean to sanctify the Lord in the eyes of others? Give a personal example from your own life.

6) What does the word *humility* really mean? Why does God often choose the "foolish things of the world"? (1 Corinthians 1:27)

7) Give a simple definition of what the "glory of God" means in Scripture. Do you find that you display the glory of God in your own life? (2 Corinthians 4:6)

Bibliography

All Biblical quotes from:

The Holy Bible: People's Parallel Edition: King James Version, New Living Translation, Tyndale House Publishers, Inc. Wheaton, Illinois, 1997.

All other references from:

Bagster, Samuel, *The Holy Vessels and Furniture of the Tabernacle of Israel,* London, England.

Barna, George, *Experiencing God in Worship,* Group, Loveland, Colorado, 2000.

Brown, Colin, *Dictionary of New Testament Theology,* Volume Two, Zondervan, Grand Rapids, Michigan, page 861.

Frangipane, Francis, *The Jezebel Spirit,* Arrow Publications, 1994.

Joyner, Rick, *Overcoming Witchcraft,* Morningstar Publications, Charlotte, North Carolina.

Missler, Nancy & Chuck, *Be Ye Transformed*, Koinonia House, Post Falls, Idaho, 1997.

Missler, Nancy & Chuck, *Faith in the Night Seasons*, Koinonia House, Post Falls, Idaho, 1997.

Missler, Nancy & Chuck, *The Way of Agape*, Koinonia House, Post Falls, Idaho, 1995.

Murray, Andrew, *The Holiest of All*, Whitaker House, New Kensington, Pennsylvania.

Richman, Chaim, *The Holy Temple of Jerusalem*, The Temple Institute, Carta, Jerusalem, 1997.

Richman, Chaim, *The Light of the Temple*, The Temple Institute, Carta, Jerusalem.

Sanders, J. Oswald, *Enjoying Intimacy with God*, Moody Press, Chicago, Illinois, 1980.

Savard, Liberty, *Shattering Your Strongholds*, Bridge-Logos Publications, Gainesville, Florida.

Smith, Alice, *Beyond the Veil*, Renew, Ventura, California.

Storge, Bob, *Exploring Worship*, Oasis House, Lee's Summit, Missouri, 2001.

Storge, Bob, *Secrets of the Secret Place,* Oasis House, Lee's Summit, Missouri, 2001.

Unger, Merrill, *Unger's New Bible Dictionary*, R.K. Harrison Edition, Moody Press, Chicago, Illinois.

Vine, W.E., *Vines Complete Expository Dictionary, Old and New Testament*, Thomas Nelson, Nashville, Tennessee, 1996.

White, John, *Pathway to Holiness*, Intervarsity Press, Downers Grove, Illinois, 1980.

Articles:

Wilkerson, David, The Pulpit Series, Times Square Church, N.Y., New York:

"The Making of a Man of God," 5/27/91
"God of the Monsters," 2/18/91
"I Almost Slipped," 3/17/97
"Stand Still and See the Salvation of the Lord," 6/9/97
"Don't Run from Jezebel," 8/2/93
"The Cost of Going all the Way with God" (no date)
"The Surrendered Life," 1/23/2002
"The Presence of God," 2/29/88
"The Manifestation of the Presence of God," 4/17/89
"The Nearness of God," 11/11/96
"Hell-Shaking Prayer," 12/18/2000

"*7000 Did Not Bow*," 4/23/2001

"*Walking in the Glory*," 3/18/99

"*Seven Women Shall Lay Hold of One Man*," 9/18/95

"*The Glory of God*," 10/16/2000

"*The Effects of Seeing the Glory of God*," 6/21/99

"*The Men Have Been With Jesus*," 9/17/2001

"*Feeding on Christ*," 2/13/2002

"*Faith Without Intimacy is no Faith at All*," 3/25/02

PLAIN & SIMPLE

Against the Tide
GETTING BEYOND OURSELVES

This little book gives the practical tools we need to implement "faith choices" in our lives. These are choices that set aside our natural thoughts and emotions, and allow us to love and be loved as God desires.

CHUCK & NANCY MISSLER

CHUCK & NANCY MISSLER

The Key
HOW TO LET GO AND LET GOD

What are the moment-by-moment steps to letting go of ourselves, our circumstances and others? How do we give our problems to God and leave them there?

Why Should I be the First to Change?
THE KEY TO A LOVING MARRIAGE

The story of the amazing "turnaround" of Chuck and Nancy's 20-year Christian marriage that reveals the dynamic secret which releases the power of God's Love already resident in every believer.

CHUCK & NANCY MISSLER

CHUCK & NANCY MISSLER

The Choice
HYPOCRISY OR REAL CHRISTIANITY

As Christians, we are faced with a constant choice: either live the Christian life in our own power and ability, or set ourselves aside and let Christ live His Life through us. One way leads to hypocrisy the other to *real* Christianity.

What is
The King's High Way?

The King's *High* Way is a ministry dedicated to encouraging and teaching Christians how to walk out their faith; i.e., focusing on the practical application of Biblical principles. Our passion is to help believers learn how to love as Jesus loved; how to renew their minds so their lives can be transformed; and, how to have unshakeable faith in their night seasons. Isaiah 62:10 is our commission: helping believers walk on the King's *High* Way by gathering out the stumbling blocks and lifting up the banner of Jesus.

For more information, please write to:

The King's *High* Way
P.O. Box 3111
Coeur d' Alene, Idaho 83816

or call:

1-866-775-KING

On the Internet:
http://www.kingshighway.org